LIVING

WITH

TEENAGERS

LIVING
WITH
TEENAGERS

Jean Rosenbaum, M.D.

Veryl Rosenbaum, Psa.

STEIN AND DAY/*Publishers*/New York

We dedicate this book to
Jessie Crawford,
a fine woman who truly understands young people.

First published in 1980
Copyright © 1980 by Jean and Veryl Rosenbaum
All rights reserved
Designed by Louis A. Ditizio
Printed in the United States of America
Stein and Day/*Publishers*/Scarborough House
Briarcliff Manor, N.Y. 10510

Library of Congress Cataloging in Publication Data

Rosenbaum, Jean.
    Living with teenagers.

    1. Adolescence. 2. Parent and child. 3. Adolescent psychology.
I. Rosenbaum, Veryl, joint author. II. Title.
HQ796.R673   306.8′7   79-3711
ISBN 0-8128-2703-1

Contents

CONTENTS

*The authors wish to acknowledge
and thank Rudite J. Emir
for her helpful meditations on this book.*

Introduction

How would you like to have these two teenagers on your hands?

She came boiling into adolescence at eleven, suddenly angry, sullen, and verbally abusive to her single-parent mother and older sister. She had been double-promoted in elementary school and thus entered high school at the age of twelve, looking fourteen or fifteen. She was obsessed with love and bullied her mother into believing she was mature enough to begin dating. During the four years of high school, she dated at least four times a week, went steady at least ten times, and had the reputation of a promiscuous girl, even though she remained a virgin. Her sex life consisted of long bouts of steamy kissing, and a very occasional light petting session. She had no knowledge of masturbation.

She had three distinct though separate personalities which she wore with ease.

At school she was the class comedienne, disrupting teachers' lectures with antics which often resulted in visits to the school counselor. This elation carried over in her relationships with girl- and boyfriends and dates. Popularity was her primary goal, and she never bothered to study, although her grades were slightly above average.

At home she was secretive, selfish (refusing to help with chores), abusive to her older sister who was a "nice" girl embarrassed by her younger sister's boisterous behavior at school. She had frequent sieges of depression when she was between boyfriends.

Her musical interest was jazz, which she played continually at incredibly loud decibel levels, not caring for the other members of the family. The only adult she felt at ease with was Jessie, the lady who cleaned the house once a week. She felt accepted by Jessie and would spend hours talking to her about life and the future—her own, of course.

She got a job at thirteen, lying about her age. She worked for three years, five hours a day, for a chiropodist as a bookkeeper, receptionist, and chair-side assistant. Her boss saw her as a shy, competent, and helpful young lady; he never knew about his young assistant's exuberant comic side, her loud mouth, or her biggest problem, drinking.

She began drinking socially at thirteen—anything, just to get drunk. She became involved with jazz musicians, many years her senior, and had bar identification (legally granted only at twenty-one) at the age of fourteen in order to quench her thirst for music and alcohol. Many of the musicians were heroin addicts, but she never felt tempted to join them.

She graduated from high school at sixteen, with the ambition to become a secretary. She studied magazines on how to dress and act like a professional secretary, and landed a job with General Motors as a private secretary to an executive. No one guessed that this sophisticated young woman was sixteen.

She was unread, uninterested in world events, and absorbed in her narrow interests. She still drank heavily. A college graduate co-worker introduced her to reading. Eventually she was encouraged to attend a night class at a city college. There she was turned on to learning and began to save money to enter college, which she did the next year.

Her attitude at home softened as she became accustomed to dealing with adults in the business world and later in college. Somehow she managed to work at three part-time jobs while carrying a full load at school.

During her first year of college she met and fell in love with a medical student. Disregarding her mother's pleas to wait, his parents' alarm, and friends' concern, she became a confident bride at seventeen. The meager finances of the newlyweds brought an end to her drinking at eighteen. She continued college and work—until she became a mother at nineteen.

As many teenage marriages do, hers failed. End of first case.

He was hurled into adolescence with grade-school-level bad behavior: stealing money from his mother's purse, slashing tires on the bikes of "enemies," making faces in class or disrupting it with imitations of a seal or horse, urinating on the radiator in the boy's bathroom. Sometimes he got caught, especially in school, which provoked visits by an embarrassed mother, laughter from his father (who himself had run away from home at fourteen), and sibling rivalry with his "good" older brother, who always aligned with the frequently hysterical mother. He earned all As in subject matter and all Fs in behavior. His only positive memories from those years were (1) a poem he wrote that was permanently posted on the school bulletin board and (2) some marble games he had invented together with his only friend.

Poorly in control at best, he was totally unprepared for the instinctual onslaught of adolescence. His response to his first masturbatory orgasm was to faint. And his response to his homosexual impulses was to engage in sexual play with every boy in the neighborhood. Because of his basic female identity vis-a-vis a father who loved him, he was able to restrain his constant rape fantasies and limit himself to endless hours of necking. When he later joined the navy at seventeen (not having finished high school), he was engaged to four girls.

His control over his aggressive impulses was totally defective and unpredictable. Having graduated from robbing mother's purse, he now tried theft from stores—clothes, food, and drinks. (The stealing of wine and whiskey led to an increasing alcoholism that reached its peak at eighteen when he was in the navy: he operated the largest still in the South Pacific.) There was also an upsurge in the quantity and quality of his malicious vandalism, such as starting fires in new houses and breaking windows.

As his creativity and intellect began to blossom, his destructiveness took new directions. His knowledge of chemistry led him to synthesize a quart of nitroglycerine, made in his basement lab from equipment partially stolen from school. He detonated part of his concoction in an alley, leveling every garage on the block and leading the local wartime weekly to speculate that the block had been subject to Japanese sabotage.

He used his intellect as a weapon, ruthlessly attacking his mediocre teachers with well-selected ideas, being very careful, however, to attack their mediocrity only within the context of the course. Though he earned all As, his attitude cost him a college scholarship. Out of bitterness he quit high school at sixteen, attended college that summer, and then joined the navy.

During those years he never once got caught by the police for any of his criminal deeds. He barely restrained himself from lethally poisoning his mother with a cyanide compound he had put together. He successfully seduced several of his brother's girlfriends. On the positive side, he came up with a number of workable inventions (including a wired chicken foot that actually walked) and wrote publishable poetry. His violent, noisy, but secretly enjoyed intellectual arguments with his self-educated father became the foundation of his later career.

These teenage "problem children" were your authors. We thought it would be helpful if parents became acquainted with our teenage years. It is amazing to us that we survived those years of reckless activities, dangerously self-destructive habits, and often inappropriate companions. Our parents are still slightly amazed that these two complicated, incorrigible kids became happy adults, healing professionals, prolific writers, and parents of five very nice children. We're kind of surprised, too.

Our own turbulent teenage years have given us special empathy for teenagers and their unique struggles. And our combined forty years of clinical practice with parents and teenagers prompt us to write this common sense guide for living with people who will be our society's future.

LIVING
WITH
TEENAGERS

ONE

The Many Hats of Parenting

Most of us cringe inwardly when parents speak baby talk to a three- or four-year-old. We wonder why they are holding back a child's verbal growth by using language unsuited to the child's developmental age. These parents have not changed their parenting hat from "infant protector" to "socializer" to fit the needs of the growing child. Their perception of the child as a sweet, adorable baby causes them to miss the signs of readiness for new possibilities in the child's expanding world.

In like manner, we often miss the emotional signs of approaching adolescence in our children, neglecting to change our approach or parenting crown from "invincible instructor" to "helpful guide" as they enter the years of individuation. Parents often unintentionally deny the obvious readiness signals because today's children enter puberty so much sooner than in the past.

Even though stages of the teenage years must be spoken of in general terms because of physical and emotional varieties, in general we can say that in previous generations puberty usually began at twelve or thirteen for girls, fourteen for boys; whereas today, girls begin adolescence anywhere from nine onward, and boys at approximately eleven. Our open-faced, guileless, innocent, adoring, playful kids are with us for a precious few years. They remain at home for many years after the beginning of adolescence, but they can no longer be thought of as simply children.

The change of hats during the teenage years is often difficult and confusing. Teenagers' swings of feelings often require parents to temporarily wear old hats from childhood, quickly shifting their approach as the teenager demands to be treated as a young adult, when the day before he may have needed parental sympathy much like a small child.

You may often feel as if you are changing roles and positions like a magician as you attempt to guide your teenagers toward adulthood. Expecting these years to be difficult and filled with challenges makes the teenage years somewhat more bearable: you know you may be called upon to modify your parenting hat daily.

Today, children are maturing physically very early, but without a concurrent escalation in emotional capacity. Though they are more knowledgeable, informed and sophisticated than the children of the past, their feelings remain at the level of their actual age.

Adolescence is the luxury of affluent societies. Before the onset of our technological age, which is a minute period in human history, children were assigned work to perform as soon as they were physically able, thus contributing their share to the survival of all. Young men and women began families of their own at fifteen or sixteen. They remained in proximity to their parents, working the same farm or else staying nearby, but they were given the respect of responsible adults. Survival precluded concern with one's internal processes.

Even today, children of poverty are forced by circumstances to grow up early and support themselves. In contrast, children of middle and upper-strata affluence remain financially and psychologically dependent upon parents many years past physical maturity. This dependence has led to the focus on adolescence as a unique phenomenon, even though people previously lived through these years without social comment. Our concern with the personality development of teenagers is a historical reaction to social change, as a technological culture has replaced the agricultural way of life.

Many writers on psychology have treated adolescence as merely a phase that people pass through, thereby reducing its significance. This approach may be reassuring to parents who feel confused and bewildered by the extremes of behavior and moods of teenagers. However, each moment of life during the adolescent years is as important to the young person as were all childhood experiences. It is of little comfort or benefit to sluff off teenage problems with the comment that "it's just a phase." Nothing feels like a phase when you are living it. One of the consistent feathers in the parenting hatband is understanding that teenagers feel they will always be inundated with excruciating sensitivity and uncontrollable mood changes. They have not yet experienced the leveling off of emotions that occurs with gradual maturity.

The adolescent years can be a profound growth experience for parents and children alike if the parents' collection of hats includes common sense, love, self-confidence, and respect when dealing with the teenagers who are trying to establish their independence from the home. Teenagers' drive toward autonomy is best understood through the family history of bonding—that profound feeling of belonging.

The three phases of the parent-child relationship are bonding, detachment, and reunion. When each phase begins and ends depends upon the unique circumstances of each family. The phases require parental intuition and knowledge about when to remove the various hats of the bonding years, exchange those during the "de-bonding" period or detachment, and be able to evolve a different style during the reunion phase.

The bonding years are when children's main source of love, approval, and acceptance rests within the family. The emotional bond which grows and develops from birth on is an intricate weave of feelings which gives children a sense of being bound together with protective, loving parents. The texture of the family bond is complex and colored by family experiences: whether the child was originally desired, if the infant and toddler was loved or disliked, if one parent is absent or withdrawn, marriage successes and failures, and the general atmosphere of acceptance in the family.

During the years when children are small, the parental hat of "protector" and "socializer" is worn in the position of a controller—children learning the rules of life in order to function inside the family and in the wider world of school and peers. The parent controls the infant's sense of well-being by dispensing love and acceptance. As the depth of the parent-child ties grows and expands the infant learns to respond to parental love. As the infant becomes a curious toddler, the parents' hats change from the "all giving" to "the demander" as they toilet train and set external controls. Children learn that cooperation, if age- and development-related, keeps them under the umbrella of bondedness.

Unavoidable parental anger and displeasure remove the sensations of safety, cause anxiety, and stimulate the child to obey family rules. As language is one of the threads of ongoing bonding, disapproving silence from a parent causes much distress in young children. The fear of parents removing the loving bonds is a controlling device for acceptable behavior which parents are often unaware of. This means of control becomes severed during the adolescent years when young people gradually and with great fluctuation debond from parents. Demanding appropriate behavior from a teenager by using the fear of bond loss is ineffective, since the teenager seeks to remove himself from the family bond in order to become independent. Other measures can be learned—exchanging the hat once again from the "hero" to the "fair advisor" in order to maintain a flow of family feelings.

The distancing from dependence during the debonding years is sometimes alarming to parents as it disrupts comfortable family routines and connections, sometimes dislodging the hat of the "controller" with a sudden jolt. In order for teenagers to successfully complete the task of puberty—becoming themselves—they must unravel their bonds with parents and learn to cope as separate people, inventing their own headgear or identity.

The process of debonding causes distress in adolescents because there are no assurances of future bonding with others during the time of breaking off emotional ties with the family. This accounts for the erratic behavior of the average teenager: The self-confident decision maker one day becomes the insecure, frightened procrastinator the next.

Teenagers debond by proclaiming their independence from parents in dress, language, and opinions. The disconnecting is apparent when teenagers seek to devalue parents—in any department. Their need to be different from their recent childishness pushes them forward, away from parents. This natural break in the cozy family bond must be made in order for teenagers to develop and grow their own sense of self. Children who cling to parents, unable or fearful of self-determination, remain childish throughout life.

Parents who deny natural debonding set up unnecessary battle-fields that teenagers must cope with, along with all the other problems of this age group. The manner in which parents react to the debonding process will determine future familial relationships. If you understand the complex tasks that confront adolescents in their struggle to achieve individual autonomy, not only will you help them reach their full potential, but also you as parents will benefit.

A mutual rebonding can occur after the young adult leaves home as a separate, no longer dependent person. However, many parents and their grown children never experience the joys of reuniting because of the rifts caused in the natural debonding years.

Sometimes rebonding occurs long after a young person has left the nest. Recently we witnessed a rebonding while waiting for a late plane in a busy metropolitan airport. We noticed a nervous couple waiting for the incoming passengers. They looked like an average middle-aged pair, except for their uptight expressions, particularly the woman's. The plane arrived, and the reason for their discomfort became apparent. Their son, whom they had obviously not seen since his marriage to a woman of another race, arrived first. He appeared anxious and concerned about how his parents would treat his wife, who made herself a shadow behind him.

Disapproval and family love flickered across the parents' faces as they saw their son. As his wife emerged, the mother-in-law tried to be gracious, but barely managed to generate kindness. The young woman then held out their baby to show her in-laws. A transformation took place as the grandmother held the infant in her arms. Her face softened, her eyes widened, and she let out a deep sigh, making an immediate generational bond with her grandchild. She started cooing loudly and began kissing the child's face. Overcome with her emotions, she laughed and cried, hugging the baby, her son, and her daughter-in-law. Grandfather too became deeply moved and joined in the celebration.

We travelers were all smiling with watery eyes as we watched this tender, intimate scene. No one could help hearing and seeing the expressions of love because all the members of the rebonding family were completely oblivious to the rest of us. It was a moment of exposed humanness, with its highest qualities revealed. The audience of strangers was enveloped with a warmth that connected all of us, for we had dropped our masks of cool urbanity and shared in the glow of a family's love.

Rebonding isn't always that dramatic, of course, but rebonding with adult offspring does give an enriched sense of generational continuum and meaning in life.

We all dream of an intact network of family with its special love components not experienced between even the closest of friends. Responsible, intelligent, and common-sense parenting brings the ultimate reward of mutual cherishment between parents and their descendants. Guilt and a constrained sense of duty are unknown in families who have sensibly survived the letting-go period of adolescence.

A Changing Life-Style

Children who grew up in the 1960s took for granted an affluent life-style. That decade offered the fulfillment of the dream of plenty. Whatever material goals anyone had were easily achievable. This way of life is coming to an abrupt halt in our time as other cultures force us into conserving energy through the pressure of the pocketbook. Our teenagers are entering a world which they are unequipped to understand or handle. We have an obligation to help them learn the ways of making do, conserving on all levels, and reducing material expectations. However, this adjustment from quantity living to quality living does not have to be sacrificial. The pleasures derived from increased personal involvement with the self and others is ultimately more rewarding than materialistic gain. Family life can become an enrichment experience once again as we are forced to spend more time and attention on interpersonal affairs.

We stand on the brink of a new way of life. Adults will have to shift learned values and become models for a simplified but rewarding life-style. Our teenagers will be listening and learning as they watch us deal with this challenge.

During the hectic, social-upheaval years of the 1960s, young adults in their twenties loudly declared their disappointment with materialistic life as they observed the lack of intimacy between parents who followed the dream of plenty, often at the expense of family closeness. They were the generation who sought answers in Eastern religion, ascetic cults, and astrology. The upcoming generation may not have the luxury of leisure time to delve into mysticism, as they will be required to devote their energies to surviving in an increasingly expensive world.

We will all be living in interesting times as our society attempts to cope with the sudden changes brought on by runaway inflation. Within this disruption, the family must survive and grow, evolving workable systems for the future.

It will probably seem to you as you continue to create workable hats and approaches to your changing teenager that you are doing most of the emotional work. As in all parenting, this is true when children are preoccupied with themselves, and assuming parents require little feedback.

The prize of parenting is that if we try to give children the opportunity to grow into loving, happy adults, they will discover their talents in order to function in our society, be able to establish relationships of love and friendship, and feel comfortable about themselves. These attributes give parents a glow of satisfaction, but the additional prize of having one's adult children as trusted friends is the most rewarding aspect of the long and often frustrating job of being a parent.

TWO

Early Female Adolescence

A group of fifth-grade children in a schoolyard usually has two or three girls who are a foot or so taller than their classmates. If a closer examination is made, these girls appear uncomfortable, slouchy, and defensive—often the result of classmates' teasing.

Children are conformists. They feel weirdly out of place when something sets them apart. Their quest for individualistic character traits, personal style, and separate opinions and ethics is not activated until late adolescence, from seventeen to twenty-one. Most youngsters even feel out of place if they have an unusual name that brings them unwanted attention. They want to hide out in the crowd. Your female author remembers, while in the third grade, insisting that her parents and friends call her Shirley Temple. She thought that if she could change her name to Shirley, people would stop teasing her about her unusual name. Of course, everyone refused to comply and teased her even more.

Early Bloomers, Late Starters

Children respond with unthinking cruelty to the girl who begins a precocious pubescent growth spurt. Girls whose bodies are still child-

11

ish are envious of the signs of change because they fear they will be left behind. Boys, already jealous about girls' freedom to feel, experience increased envy when girls begin to mature faster than they do. These jealousies cause the smaller children to taunt the taller, bust-and-buttock-developing girl, who may be only ten years old.

Even if the early bloomer uses indifference as a defense against her tormentors, she suffers inwardly and feels abnormal. She may cover up her breast development by wearing voluminous blouses, or walk with her shoulders hunched over to reduce the size of her bust. If there are several girls who suddenly begin to look like young women, they will cling together for support. Such a mini-club can be most reassuring to girls who have jumped ahead of the group. They will feel a kinship because of their similarities in tribulation. In order to compensate for peer rejection, these early starters often wear a mask of superiority, trying for pseudo-sophistication. The year or two of being different can leave a girl wounded and unhappy, even though her female classmates will soon catch up.

Mini-clubs often consist of three or four girls who consider each other best friends. The members of the club form revolving cliques, which often leave one girl out for a short time.

Mrs. March found her thirteen-year-old daughter, Gail, in a despairing state, crying because her two girlfriends had told her that no one liked her. This announcement came after they had been giggling and congratulating Gail about her winning a ribbon in a horse show.

"My first instinct was to call up those mean friends of Gail's and tell them they were jealous little sneaks. I'm discovering that jumping in to protect my child is only a form of interference. I listened sympathetically and explained that maybe her friends felt a little bad because she had won something. This had never occurred to her. That night, Gail was back 'in' and gabbing on the phone with one of her buddies. If I had gotten involved with her spats and tried to mediate, I would most likely have made her 'out' stage last longer."

Mrs. March learned that when young teenagers hurt each other's feeling, they usually do not hold grudges as adults do. They quickly forgive and forget slights in order to get back inside their peer groups. Parents often have a difficult time maintaining the understanding-observer position, but these lessons in relating are a part of learning to deal with people. Because of their very youth, resilient teenagers bounce back from rejection, and eagerly rejoin the friends who recently treated them insensitively.

Three girls who begin to play together because of their early development helped each other with such loving support that they remain friends to this day, when all now are in their thirties. They practiced growing-up rituals by taking turns applying makeup on each other, trying glamorous hairstyles, teaching each other to dance, and spending endless hours pondering what intercourse would be like. They shared all their secrets, crushes on older boys, and fantasies about how each boy would kiss. Soon after saying good-bye, they would be stretched out over chairs, legs dangling, whispering further secrets into the telephone.

They were inseparable through junior and senior high school. Their bonds were so close that no jealousies ever existed among the three girls, even though their talents, looks, and financial conditions were quite different. They shared clothes and information, and helped with advice and concern whenever one or the other was heartbroken over a boy. The first girl to have intercourse immediately shared her reactions with her eager and curious friends.

Other girls, attracted to this group of special, bonded friends, often tried to join their triad. But the girls had an unwritten, secret language, which they had created in grade school and which they refused to explain to anyone. Whenever another girl persisted in her attempts to become accepted, the girls would begin to speak in their secret language, signaling one of them to take the girl aside. She would then explain with great seriousness that they were lesbians and that homosexuality was catching. This maneuver frightened away those seeking membership in their inner circle, and caused great merriment for the three. They were so comfortable with their sexual identity that the thought of anyone actually believing their story was extremely hilarious to the ebullient bunch.

They all had a sense of the absurd and were popular, funny people. They created comedy acts which they performed in school programs.

Even when they married, they maintained contact, apart from their husbands. Today, separated by career moves, they meet yearly, and each time they do, they feel as if they had been together just last week.

Their bonds of friendship, begun out of shared adversity, have been a sustaining force throughout their lives—through the death of parents, birth of children, divorce, and other good and bad fortune.

In order to lend emotional support to precocious girls, parents can foster activities that help them feel at ease with their new contours. Early starters hear enough comments from insensitive adults—"My, how you've grown!"—to have to deal with parental teasing or disinterest. They are keenly aware of their new bodies and feel estranged enough from their former physiques.

A nine-year-old daughter of one of our clients requested a meeting. She wanted to know why her eleven-year-old sister had changed so suddenly. Previously they had gotten along well—sharing a bedroom, giggling, playing, and being friends. "Now all she does is pick on me and threaten me by saying she'll never talk to me again and that I'll shrivel up and die."

After being assured that she would not die if her sister didn't speak to her, we asked the little girl to help us find the cause for her sister's sudden hatefulness. After some dead-end exploring, the girl mentioned that her sister recently gave up going to their gymnastic classes. "She just got too tall all of a sudden and can't do the flips and stuff as good as me." We suggested that maybe her sister was jealous since she couldn't perform like her petite sister. "How could an older sister ever be jealous of me?" asked the surprised child. When she understood how a spurt in growth can make someone feel awkward and thus jealous, she was most sympathetic. "Now that I know the reason, I'm sorry for her. I won't tell her I know, but I'll feel better."

A mother's relaxed attitude and availability for information can ease the transition from a childhood body to the new figure of a young woman. In an attempt to be modern, some mothers go overboard and continue asking their daughters about their most intimate feelings. Such questioning makes girls feel invaded and resentful. They need time and experience to absorb the plethora of new information and also to become accustomed to body changes. The young value a mother's respect for privacy.

We received this letter from a confused mother:

Dear Rosenbaums,
    My thirteen-year-old daughter Jennifer has always been

close to me. My husband and I have four boys, and another female in the family has always been a delight for me. We never seemed to have the problems which plagued many of my friends and their girls. It seemed to me that a lot of mothers and daughters are competitive, always niggling at each other.

Jennifer always confided in me, came to me with her questions and sought solace by my side when her brothers' teasing was too heavy-handed.

Her sudden antagonism toward me seems to have sprung up overnight. Now, she shares her confidences with her girlfriends and her diary. She moves her face when I attempt to kiss her, looks exasperated when I ask about school (she called me The Who-What-Where-Why Lady yesterday), and has suddenly become embarrassed about my auto mechanic's job even though I've been one for five years and she used to bring her friends to watch me work. Now, I'm "unfeminine, nosy and gushy." This all makes me feel inferior as a mother, and like I'm losing a companion. The ridiculous thing is that two of my boys have already passed through the stage of moving away from me as "The Mommy Person" and I hardly even noticed them backing off. They tease me and call me old-fashioned, but their veiled criticisms don't sting me like Jennifer's coolness. When she joins her brothers in their teasing, I feel betrayed, like she's gone over to their camp. I had thought we would become even closer during her teen years. What have I done to cause this hostility? My husband thinks all the kids are fine and says I worry too much.

Jennifer was reacting normally to the instinctual push to debond from her mother. The woman's desire to become closer during the teen years clashed with the daughter's need to put some distance between the generations. Jennifer had to equate their palship with her childhood, and thus sought to shut off all their "traditions"— confiding, us-against-the-brothers, pride in her mother's job, affection, and sharing the day's activities.

It was almost as if mother and daughter were too close, much like girlfriends. The shock of the daughter's removal from the circle of two females was abrupt. She was rejecting the pleasant, past relationship which was no longer comfortable. It was a signal for the mother to begin relating on a different level.

The mother wrote again, a year later, relating how she realized she had wanted to keep Jennifer as a little sister. She stopped questioning her daughter and discovered that without her inquisitive approach Jennifer volunteered conversation. She confessed that she was jealous of the closer feelings between the brothers and Jennifer, but understood that it was healthier for her daughter than remaining a little girl. She related that she and her daughter developed a new, grown-up ritual which they both enjoyed. They spent morning time together, sharing the bathroom mirror as they applied their make-up. "We feel close and comfortable doing something which doesn't remind Jennifer of her childish attachment of the past."

Many mothers have related that the first step away from them usually caused feelings of rejection. Once they learned to not take this move toward becoming separate as personal, but rather as a growth phenomena, they could enjoy watching their daughter's independence blossom.

The girl who appears to lag behind in physical development needs support also. Her more mature friends may ignore her, treating her as if she were still a baby. She will feel rejected and confused, thinking her time will never arrive. Her mother or a trusted pediatrician can assure her that her maturation will indeed happen, only at her own internal pace. Since children still retain views of godlike parental power, some girls feel angry at their mothers for their delayed puberty, as if the mother were responsible for their slow rate of growth.

"I think that the two years I still looked like a little girl while my classmates were all lithe and lean were the loneliest years of my life," reported a high school senior. "I felt angry at my old friends because of their silly secrets and dumb talk about movie stars. I still wanted to play Monopoly but they refused to play that silly old game. I had an imaginary companion whom I called 'Talky.' She sat on my shoulder, and we had long conversations about how mean everyone was to me. She loved me, and everything I did was just fine with her.

"My mother kept saying, 'You'll catch up,' which didn't help me at all. I accused her of doing something deliberate to stunt my growth.

Talky and books saved me from total desolation. When I finally started to lose my baby fat and grow and menstruate, I gave a big party just to announce to my old girlfriends that I was a woman, too. I wrote a story about being short, and lagging behind, and how kids can make up fantasy friends to help out. It was published and sent to the junior high schools in my city. A lot of kids called me and thanked me for reminding them that they were okay."

Learning About the Body and Its Changes

Since our children live inside their bodies, we want them to feel good about their internal workings. Education about the body should also include information about feelings stirred up by the beginning of puberty.

The Onset of Menstruation
The physical indicators of puberty occur in girls before they begin menstruation. These signals of readiness mark the time for parental discussion and preparation.

Generally, we believe that mothers should explain menstruation to girls. Many twelve- and thirteen-year-old girls are shy and wildly embarrassed about their changing bodies. Even if the physical description of menstruation has been detailed in sex-education classes, girls like to hear about "what it's really like" from another woman they feel close to.

"My daughter was uncomfortable when I began our conversation about her future periods," reports Mrs. Hicks. "I felt frustrated with her. I had resolved to enlighten her, because I had been deprived of information as a youngster. I thought my openness would free her spirit and somehow relieve her of all the worries I had as a young girl. Her main concern was if her father had to know and if boys would be able to tell when she was bleeding. She had heard older boys teasing girls about 'being on the rag,' and feared they would torment her. My main job seemed to be to listen to her fears about people knowing because the actual workings of the uterus didn't concern her.

"I learned from that experience to look for what *she* needed, not to try to make up for what *I* lacked as an adolescent. I think it would have been a big mistake if my husband had been there at our initial talk, since she was leary of the male attitude. When she began her periods, she proudly announced it to both her dad and myself. You might think that the opposite of what to expect, but teenagers are always surprising you. We both congratulated her and it was all very natural."

Other young girls have been raised in families where both parents have been answering questions about sex and growth since childhood. If the girl feels relaxed, already discussing sex changes in front of her father, then menstruation can easily be approached together. As with Mrs. Hicks, you may discover that the questions surrounding menstruation will be about feelings connected with the process, rather than the physical and biological facets of menarche.

The beginning of menstruation has great psychological significance to girls, as it heralds the biological beginning of their womanhood. If the mother buys a book on menstruation and drops it on her daughter's lap, the girl will think that the mother is uneasy about body functions. Such action confuses girls, making them wonder why something described as normal is being treated secretively.

Books on menstruation can be valuable if read together and used as a springboard for questions and answers. If you think that children will naturally learn about menstruation from friends, you are correct. However, myths and scary stories still flourish in our supposedly educated and liberated society. One teenager thought that every time she bled, a baby was being destroyed. She heard this explanation from a trusted friend and naturally believed the account, since the menstrual flow proved that something was bleeding. She felt remorse and guilt during every menstrual period, for she thought she was responsible for the murder of a baby. It is easier to prepare and educate young girls about the mechanics of menstruation than to allow them to be burdened with nonsensical misinformation gleaned from friends or their vivid imaginations.

Menstruation can be explained in a clear and concise manner by treating it as a monthly occurrence that females must deal with for approximately thirty years. If mothers describe the menses as natural, instead of as an illness, girls can treat the process casually. They usually worry about being caught without supplies when menstruation begins. The first experience need not be one of embarrassment if mothers make sure that supplies are readily available. Some misled girls think that a torrent of blood will come whooshing down their legs, and they wait with great anxiety for the first period. Other young girls, in their eagerness to belong, pretend that they have begun menstruation before they actually have. They long to participate in this symbolic passage into womanhood and think it is a badge of honor.

Menstruation can be thoroughly but simply explained so that a girl fully understands what occurs to her internally. The simplest explanation is that the ovaries, two almond-shaped glands situated on either side of the uterus, become stimulated by hormones and begin to manufacture tiny eggs. As an egg begins to ripen, the uterus lining thickens and stores up blood which would nourish the egg if it were fertilized. (Most children understand fertilization, but this is a good time to explain that a male sperm causes the egg to become a fetus.)

One ovary then releases the ripened egg in a process called ovulation, which occurs about halfway through the twenty-eight day female reproductive cycle, or approximately fourteen days after the beginning of the previous menstrual period. When the egg leaves the ovary, it is caught in a tube (Fallopian). As the egg floats down the tube toward the uterus, it can be fertilized by a sperm. If fertilization happens, the egg lodges itself in the thickened lining of the uterus. If the egg is not fertilized, it shrivels up and leaves the body with the menstrual flow. The blood is shed because it is not needed to nurture the egg.

Such an explanation adequately describes the reason for menstruation. Drawings or a book with simple pictures can be helpful aids. Some girls become irritated and want to know why menstruation has to happen if they're not going to have a baby for many years or maybe never. Telling them that body functions happen outside the realm of personal plans helps them accept the reality of their physical make-up.

Menstruation does not have to interfere with normal activities. Reassuring the premenstrual girl that her life will go on as usual can relieve worries. She should also be prepared for the fact that her first period will probably be slight and that a regular rhythm will not establish itself until about a year after the flow begins. This caution will alleviate fears that can occur when periods are missed in the beginning year. Young girls, in their secret conversations, can convince each other that sperm can be transmitted by kissing, holding hands, sharing toilet seats used by males, and by any other method that tickles their fanciful imaginations.

In the case of menstruation, as with all sexual matters, the mother's attitude toward her own body and sexuality will profoundly influence the daughter's feelings about her femininity. With the onset of puberty and menstruation, the sexual feelings and urges are heightened. Girls will want to know about masturbation and what personal stance they should take.

"I hate the word masturbation. It sounds wrong," says Marylou. "I looked it up in the dictionary and it said, 'stimulation of the sexual organs, usually by oneself.' That sounded icky, but then it said, 'also called onanism, self-abuse.' That really scared me! I asked my Mom what self-abuse was and she gave me a long lecture on certain religious cults who flagellate themselves. I wondered if flagellation was the same as masturbating, but was too confused to ask any more."

Young people, fearful of appearing naive, or responding to an unspoken repressive atmosphere about sex, will use the dictionary as a last resort. Even though we have ample literature on sexuality which clearly states that masturbation is healthy, our generation was brought up by parents who thought it was dirty and that men did "it," but rarely women. These beliefs may still lurk under the surface of today's modern parents and even though you might say that masturbation is normal, you may not feel that it is really natural.

"I'm trying to educate my two girls, unlike my mother who never said a word but just looked pained when sexual matters were mentioned. We were talking about sexuality in both men and women, and masturbation came up. I explained that sexual feelings are present from birth to old age and that people are not sexually active just between twenty and thirty, but that it is a human appetite, always present, revealing itself in different forms.

"Babies are sensually happy with sucking and stroking. Children love and need affection. Teenagers are able to have intercourse, but I feel they should wait until they are older and can handle the emotions which come with sexual intimacy. I explained that touching and rubbing one's clitoris feels good, orgasms relieve normal tensions, and it's a healthy outlet for sexual feelings. Everything was fine until my fourteen-year-old, Brenda, asked me if I had played with myself when I was their age. I hadn't expected such a personal question and was taken aback.

" 'Mom, you want us to talk about our feelings, why shouldn't you tell us about yours?'

"She was right. I said I had felt so guilty about touching myself that I had never actually masturbated in a straight-forward manner. I remembered pressing my legs together and feeling warm sensations.

"They wanted to know if I masturbated now. I had a vivid fantasy of wanting to say, 'Well, that's enough for now, we'll talk about it later.' I pushed on and explained that I didn't feel the need because I was sexually satisfied with my husband.

" 'But, if it's normal and healthy, why not do both?' they wondered, kind of disbelieving that their father and I were sexually active.

"We left it that some married people probably enjoy masturbation as well as intercourse, and it's up to everyone to decide what is pleasurable. I couldn't tell them that even if I were alone I don't think I would masturbate. The taboo for me is still present. I certainly want them to be more at ease with their bodies than I was, so I don't feel like I'm saying, 'Do what is healthy, but don't use me as a model!' I'm telling them that sexual mores change with the generations. My younger daughter, twelve, decided she wasn't even interested in having an orgasm that way, but thought the whole subject was keen."

Most people have fantasies while masturbating and it is helpful to talk about the fun of fantasies as harmless free-flowing imaginative creativity. Girls usually fantasize a romantic setting—a cozy cabin, a mellow fire, candles and soft music playing as a smooth and confident lover slowly and thoughtfully seduces them. They are often shocked when the boys they date fall short of their daydreams of the romantic approach.

"Most boys are into the fast grope, which is totally repulsive," stated Fredrica at a teenage seminar on feelings.

"We just get real excited," countered one of her male classmates.

"That's just a cop-out because you don't care about the girl's feelings. How would you like it if some girl you just met grabbed your private parts and started leering at you?"

Although Fredrica's turning-the-tables example caused laughter, she made the boys think about how it might feel to be treated as a thing, rather than a person with sensitive feelings.

Another boy explained that he was afraid girls would laugh at him if he tried to be romantic.

"Well, none of us know anything yet. We should try to learn how to be thoughtful together," spoke another student.

Sometimes girls will have sexual fantasies about being forced into intercourse by a strong-willed man who renders them helpless to resist. This can be alarming if a girl thinks she may have some hidden desire to be raped.

Reassurance can be given by explaining that these kinds of fantasies are an attempt to deny one's normal wishes for sex by having the fantasy male figure take all the responsibility. The girl in the fantasy is innocent because she is the victim rather than admitting her own sexual feelings.

The more reassuring parents can be about the normalcy of strange fantasies and daydreams, the more children will feel relaxed and not think they are going crazy—one of the major worries of teenagers.

Questions About Reproduction

If your daughter asks some stumping questions about her reproductive organs, learn together by reading books or asking someone who is better informed. Children feel inferior when parents act as if they know everything. Any question children ask about sexuality is a barometer of their readiness to know. If parents assure children that any and all queries will be answered, they pick up the attitude that sex is healthy and not tinged with mystery.

Simple, straightforward answers are better than long, involved explanations. A woman who had made a pact with herself to prepare and inform her daughters about sexual matters went overboard. When a television announcer discussed an epidemic of syphilis, her two girls asked for an explanation. The mother turned off the television, called in the father and had him grimly explain the reproductive systems of the male and female, using language and technical terms which neither youngster could comprehend. The girls would have been satisfied with a simple explanation of how germs can cause disease.

The father ended the discussion by telling his daughters that if they ever were in trouble (not explained) when they were with a boy (they hadn't even thought about dating), they could always call home for help. They were too unsettled to ask what kind of trouble the father might be talking about. As it was, the ten-year-old somehow came away from the discussion with a notion that the man eats a special kind of bread to make sperm and then feeds this concoction to his wife. She stopped eating bread for several months.

The physical changes that should be explained and discussed with early adolescent girls are: the growth of the breasts accompanied by nipple growth with dark circles, or areolas, around the nipples that puff up, sometimes causing sensitivity. Hips begin to round out as a result of the broadening of the bony pelvis and the deposition of subcutaneous fat. Her legs lengthen, which adds to her height. Pubic and auxilliary hair appear along with the further development of the labia and clitoris. Explaining what young girls can expect in bodily changes eases any alarm that they may be "different" from other females.

The Need to Feel in Control

In order to be in control of *something,* many early adolescent girls between nine and twelve become obsessed with horses. They devote hours to lessons, riding, and shows, and spend many more grooming their beloved animals. The rigid rules of horse-care, management, and tournament procedures give them some structure to depend on. They can count on the performance of a well-trained horse much more than on their own feelings. If parents can afford this hobby, it's a healthy outlet for exercising external controls, as is any other activity which enhances a feeling of achievement.

A professional photographer related that when she was a teenager she felt irritated and goofy when her limbs started to sprout. She became obsessed with her growing nose, which was all she could see for a long time. As she was continually watching her nose, she kept bumping into walls, door frames, and her parents. "One day, my dad brought home a camera and announced that it was for me. He taught me how to use it and turned my gruesome attention from my nose to something really exciting and interesting. He was a sweet person who never got annoyed at my strange behavior, but just kindly revealed to me that the world was bigger than my nose. He actually handed me my career that day."

Insightful parents understand that young girls often suffer with the ups and downs of their feelings, and will invest, temporarily, all of their love on a domestic animal, such as a cat or dog. These pets are safer to deal with than parents and peers, as they give unconditional love reminiscent of childhood.

Fathers and Daughters

Fathers have a complicated responsibility as their daughters begin to mature physically. Girls usually have a deep emotional bond with their dads, idealizing them as superheroes. This mutual bond is inter-woven and infused with sensual attachments. Little girls compete for the father's attention, having the self-delusional fantasy that they would be better wives than their mothers. Even though their interests become outer-directed during the grade-school years, girls are still very attached to their fathers. The father's love and approval are extremely important, since his affectionate attention validates the girl's lovability.

A father related to us that he was confronted by a business friend about his handling of his twelve-year-old daughter: "You know, you talk about her as though she's still a little girl. Have you really looked at her lately?" He hadn't. He kept a picture of her in his wallet: she was seven, dressed in a ballerina's tu-tu, looking sweet, innocent, and asexual. It occurred to him that his daughter was frozen in his memory as that adorable little dancer and that he always thought of her that way. He had no such frozen memory of his older boys. "I was just protecting myself by denying that my sweet little princess was grow-ing up. She must have felt as though I was some kind of clown when I kept asking her how her dancing was doing. She'd look disdainfully at me and say, 'Oh, dad, I gave that up two years ago!' The night after my friend confronted me, I really looked at her and saw how lovely she was. When I told her what a fine young lady she was becoming, she lit up like a Christmas tree.

"We started talking, and I learned how interested she was in solar energy. She taught me how we could inexpensively use the sun to heat a part of our house. She had a system worked out for blowing the heat from the attic into various rooms. Her enthusiasm, brightness, and creativity came pouring out as she shared her ideas with me. It's as if I woke up to find a delightful person who had replaced my outdated image of my little dancer. We have remained close ever since, because I praise and validate her mind, her graceful good looks, and her wonderful spirit. I often think what joys of fathering I would have missed if that friend of mine hadn't told me off."

The sudden changes in a girl's body push her to seek confirmation from her father. Many men feel uncomfortable as they watch the daughter's body grow into that of a young woman. The arrival of another woman in the house stimulates adult sexual feelings. The daughter, who sees parents as loving but essentially asexual, has no awareness of her impact on her father.

Men who experience guilt about these normal reactions often abruptly withdraw their affection from their budding girls. They feel at a loss about how to behave, cover up their sexual arousal, and retreat behind a cold front. This sudden switch confuses the young-ster and makes her feel rejected and worthless. One girl compared such rejection to being suddenly dropped from a high precipice after having felt safe in her father's love. The bond is broken as if by a surgical procedure. Since childhood experiences of bond loss occur when children misbehave, the young teenage girl assumes the bond removal is associated with her new sexual appearance, which she now translates as "bad."

Fathers should feel free to discuss these strange new feelings with their wives or, if single, with empathetic friends. Honest men will quickly share similar disquieting experiences. Knowing that this reac-tion is normal and that it also occurs between mothers and sons gives family sexual attraction its proper perspective. Overt seduction does not have to occur just because a person feels stimulated by a relative's body. Feelings of guilt and shame evaporate with mature acceptance of sexual arousal and the decision to sublimate those feelings. Under-standing wives can casually teach their daughters to wear a robe around the house. Most girls feel modest about their new bodies anyway and do not flaunt themselves.

Sometimes, a girl will be completely unaware of her impact on parents. A mother reported how her daughter's newly developing body had made the older woman feel inferior. The mother was tall and thin, whereas her teenage daughter's body was very buxom. The girl enjoyed being so well endowed and refused to wear a bra. "Her breasts were beautiful, and the thinner the tee shirt, the better she liked it. She loved the attention men gave her, and with her sexy glances, she got plenty of adoration. I caught myself feeling jealous and picking on her for her lack of modesty. She told me I was old-fashioned and that none of her friends squeezed themselves into weird, unnatural shapes with bras. I had to deal with the silly old cultural notion that large breast size equals sexuality, something I thought was resolved in my young adulthood. It's another matter when you have a daughter sharing the limelight in your own house. I was really feeling competitive with her for my husband's approval. I was too embarrassed to confess these feelings to my mate.

"I love my daughter, and we have always been close, so I decided to talk with her. She is intelligent and sensitive. When I told her how I felt, she was surprised that an adult would experience feelings of inadequacy. She put her arms around me and said, 'You're the most beautiful person I know. You just made me feel like a friend instead of a kid. Do you think daddy notices my figure too?' I told her that the reason her father hid behind the paper was that he didn't know where to look when she came bounding in with her sheer tee-shirts. 'You mean I make him uncomfortable too!?'"

The girl, enjoying her new curves, had no idea that she could arouse sexual feelings in her stodgy-looking father. She decided to cover up, "just a little," to ease the tension. Her mother and she developed a sisterly feeling for each other after the exchange of personal confidences, and the father came out of hiding when his daughter toned down her dress and posturing. Her mother said, "I learned a big lesson when I opened up my feelings to my daughter. She could empathize on a very mature level. I really gave her an opportunity to prove how she cared for us, and she came through in a splendid fashion."

A father can create new ways in which to reveal his continued love and approval of his daughter and her growing femininity. Kisses on the cheek and a warm, quick hug accompanied with some compliment keep the bond alive. Lap sitting can be discouraged by lightly commenting that the daughter is getting too heavy for the old man to hold. A father's interest in and willingness to talk about, his daughter's activities are tangible signs of love and acceptance.

During a lecture on fathers and daughters, a woman shared a ritual her father had devised when his girls began their adolescence. He had written them a letter which she said had made her and her sisters feel special and deeply loved. She had saved hers and shared his thoughtful words with the listeners:

Dear Dorothy,

You are beginning your unique transformation from girlhood to womanhood. As your father I will proudly watch your adventures with self-discovery, love, creativity, and career choices, as well as your approach to the good and bad experiences which will surely happen in your life.

I promise you these things:

I will let you choose your friends without making judgments. This is difficult for a father to do, because we hate to see our daughters hurt by people we know are uncaring. I will allow you to learn for yourself whom to trust and in whom to invest your loyalties.

I will respect your privacy, knocking before I enter your room. Your emotional privacy will also be treated with dignity, because I will not pry when you need solitude.

I will give you advice, but only when you ask for it.

If you make mistakes, which of course you will, I will be a friend and not criticize your blunders.

I will listen to you about your feelings, opinions, and criticisms. I will make every effort to understand you.

When you fall in love, I will not be jealous when your boyfriend claims your heart.

I will encourage you to reach the potential of your emotional, intellectual, creative and spiritual possibilities.

I have expectations for your happiness. As I have watched you grow, I have observed your special gift to make people laugh at life. I hope you always retain your joyful spirit. You have gifts which I dream will enrich your life. I expect you will become a remarkable person.

I will ask you to consider some promises I would like you to make to yourself:

Be always open to new people, shunning familiar sameness.

Be curious about the world.

Be curious about yourself and learn the poetry of your heart.

Be proud of yourself when you must make decisions which go against the flow.

Be honest with yourself.

As you become yourself, please remember that love is the center of a happy, fulfilling life. If you love yourself and others as deeply as I love you, you will be the person I know is emerging from my little girl.

Your Dad

After the woman finished the letter, she said that throughout her adolescence she was inspired to live up to her father's expectations. "They gave meaning to my life then and still do."

This father lent the occasion of puberty a special sense of refinement.

Fathers who repress their sudden sexual feelings may become angry at their daughters for stimulating these responses. It is not the child's fault that her body is growing, just nature following its inevitable course. Suspicion about her behavior with boys is only avoiding the real issue.

A woman related how her father started giving her lectures when she was nine. He would angrily denounce her for looking intently at men. Out of fear of punishment, she lied to him pretending not to know what he was talking about. In fact, she was extremely curious about and attracted to all men and couldn't wait to grow up and start kissing—her nine-year-old version of adult sexuality.

Her father always seemed to be watching her and had some critical remark to make about her appearance. She grew more and more resentful of his invasions into her life. She was a pretty girl and a superb athlete. When she was eleven, boys started coming by the house, but for the next three years, her father refused to allow her to go anywhere at night with boys. He grew increasingly agitated as more and more boys came to talk, play cards, and grab a kiss or two when the "Lurker" (as they called him) wasn't around.

When she was about to begin high school, he gave a crushing edict: she was not going to be allowed to date until she was seventeen, the year she would graduate. He had not given the same harsh directive to his two older daughters, and the budding teenager knew he was afraid of her sexual interests. She tried prevailing on her mother to change the unfair rule, but the father would not listen to any arguments in the girl's favor.

"I hated him so much for trying to own me. I had fantasies of his dying in many gruesome ways. The awful thing is that he did die, two months after he set down the rule for my not dating. I was convinced that I had caused his fatal heart attack because of my murderous wishes. I lived with that guilt until I went into analysis years later. My analyst revealed to me that my father was obviously sexually attracted to me and projected his feelings into suspicions about my sexual plans. I had a lot of unresolved anger toward him, but analysis helped me purge myself of those feelings. I can honestly say that if he had lived, he would have made me miserable, and I'm sure I would have rebelliously married very young, just to get away from his grip."

The Shifted Idol

Young pubescent girls are much too interested in their own bodies, feelings, and dreams to give much time to boys. Besides, they have no males to choose from, as their classmates are still childish and senior-high boys are involved with their own age group. Many girls in early adolescence direct their new sexual and romantic stirrings to mass adoration of the current popular musician, TV, or movie star. They become frantically enthusiastic about their idol's every statement, record, or personal performance. They feel betrayed if their fantasy lover announces his marriage. As they still want to conform to the herd, friends are sought with similar heroes. They feel normal if they all can swoon and shriek over the same object of their unrequited love. These daydream crushes are safe and perfectly normal.

The romanticized love they once felt for their fathers is transferred to the elusive entertainment idol in an exaggerated form. Their new feelings of love constitute their first step in debonding from the father. The father who feels irritated with the daughter's hysterical obsession with an idol must examine his hidden feelings of jealousy. He is losing the kingly position enjoyed during his daughter's infancy and juvenile years. This shift has to happen in order for her eventually to form intimate love relationships outside the family bond. Her feelings for her father are still present, but overshadowed by the fascination with the celebrity.

Barbara's father received news of a promotion and called his wife at her office to announce the family would celebrate by going to an exclusive restaurant for dinner that evening. She was excited and thrilled, called home to tell Barbara not to begin dinner as they would all be eating out. Barbara, fourteen, was unimpressed and wanted to stay home and "goof around." "Besides, Mom, I don't want to get dressed and sit at a dumb table for two hours. Ann and Chris are coming over anyway. We have to study for a test. I just can't go."

The adults felt their daughter didn't care about their success and happiness, even though she would share in the new advantages of the promotion. They talked about it over dinner and Mr. Doran had an insight. "We hadn't taken into account that her idol is a millionaire and has achieved the top at the age of twenty-two, and in a field that excites and interests Barbara. How could she be thrilled that I'm now an executive in an engineering firm? To her that's dull work compared to a singer. I had to face my feelings of competition for my daughter's hero worship. I didn't even know I had them until I felt somewhat deflated that she wanted to stay home instead of celebrating with us. A year ago it would have been different, but that was then."

Mr. Doran was willing to examine his reactions before jumping on his daughter with guilt maneuvers of "you act like you're not a part of this family," or "you're going with us and that's final." This would only result in a sullen teenager who would ruin the evening, acting like a prisoner on a leash. He didn't insist on controlling her and even though she would take his attitude for granted, her right to choose was left intact.

A thirteen-year-old girl asked, "I babysit for a couple with three kids. They go out at least twice a week. They're about thirty, I think. What kind of fun can they be having at their age?"

She really saw them as over the hill. Her classmates nodded in agreement. We asked how they viewed their fathers—as old fogies or able to still enjoy fun and romance. After some giggling, they commented,

"I used to think dad was Superman, but now he's always tired."

"I feel embarrassed when my parents start getting mushy. Isn't that just for young people?"

"My dad keeps talking about the Korean war as if it were yesterday. He's got a box of medals he always wants to show my friends. I could just die!"

"My dad's okay. He lets me have my friends over any time as long as we're not too loud. But he thinks everything's too noisy. Is that how old people are?" Her father is thirty-six.

The fantasy life that revolves around the sympathetic, all-accepting vocalist or movie star makes up for the lack of boy-girl friendships during this time.

Mrs. Erickster found herself increasingly irritated with her thirteen-year-old daughter, Jill covered her bedroom walls with pictures of her singing idol, listened constantly to his tapes and could not concentrate on her schoolwork, conversations with parents, or remember to keep promises—just like anyone who is in love.

"I'm a working person, besides running our household, and am busy beyond belief. All this mooning about her hero seemed ridiculous to me. One night I was complaining to my husband after Jill had 'forgotten' to start dinner because she and her friends were writing fan letters. My husband has an impy sense of humor. He quietly picked out a record and played a Sinatra song, just looking at me with a wry smile. I had totally forgotten that I had been a 'swooner' and had been crazy about Frankie, as we lovingly called him. My husband had a good laugh on me, but his humorous approach helped me understand Jill's obsession.

"I had amnesia about my teenage feelings. Maybe we all put those years in a private, sealed place and forget them. They were so painful most of the time. I knew Jill wouldn't believe that I had experienced the same intense longings as she was feeling for her singer so I didn't try to be her pal. Instead I wrote down a story about a lovelorn girl who plots to meet Frank Sinatra. It helped me understand Jill and not feel so condescending. I decided to try to recall my adolescent years whenever she latches onto some other strange behavior and try to be more empathetic."

The Creative Child

Some children do not make attachments to movie or singing idols, animals, or close friends. They may prefer to direct their time and energies to creative gifts and talents. They have the inner resources and the drive of creativity to support them through the first years of physical and emotional changes. Creativity flourishes in solitude, and parents should respect the need for aloneness in creative children, not forcing them into social activities which they may find boring and nonproductive.

The Parents' Role

Parental support and validation are vital when a girl begins the lengthy process of growing into a woman. It seems to the youngster that she has just learned the necessary controls to handle school and social skills in grade school when her body begins all sorts of sudden changes over which she has no control.

An eleven-year-old girl who had been in ballet classes for six years complained that, suddenly, every time she got out of the car she whacked her head. "Am I becoming a total jerk, or what?" she asked her mother, really disgusted with her clumsiness. Her mother explained to her that she just hadn't gotten comfortable with her new size and was misjudging the height of the car door. When the girl realized that this simple observation was indeed true, she paid more attention when judging heights and stopped bumping into things. She regained her bodily self-esteem because her mother was willing to help her figure out what was going on.

Instead of becoming irritated with her daughter's accidents, the mother took time to consider her daughter's changes and consequent physical bumblings. A great number of irritating or annoying habits of teenagers can actually be understood and explained when one considers the adjustment they are trying to make to their new bodies and feelings.

So much of parenting during the teen years requires this kind of patient awareness of children's confusion.

THREE

Early Male Adolescence

The Emotional Jolt

Boys impatiently await their adolescent growth spurt as they witness their female classmates' physical changes. The approximately two year earlier maturation in girls often escalates boys' pre-existing, although denied, jealousy of the opposite sex.

Boys carry a psychological burden throughout their developmental years. Their burden is a culturally imposed view of masculinity and the resultant role expectations.

Little boys, usually until the toddler stage, are allowed to express their feelings. They can cry, show alarm, be affectionate, gentle, and cling to parents for security. Often before three, boys are admonished, threatened, and pressured into blocking out the majority of their natural feelings. Boys who cry are called sissies. The intuitive mechanism, a human non-sex-related trait, which requires sensitive awareness to feeling reactions about people and events, is labeled feminine. Showing fear is frowned upon, as is enjoying passive play. The "all boy" is outgoing, stoic, competitive, and displays no soft or tender qualities. In contrast, girls are encouraged to be comfortable with their feelings.

The guides for masculinity are integrated into a boy's view of appropriate behavior by the time he enters grade school. Because the

33

lessons to conform to the masculine image are automatically taught, we may assume these are easy tasks for the youngster to master. However, it requires a tremendous amount of internal and external control to repress normal feelings.

Boys are angry that they must learn to control and hide feelings which were once acceptable. They observe other children (girls) expressing themselves, and naturally feel envious. After repeatedly hearing that feelings are sissified and inappropriate, boys gradually begin to think that their automatic emotional responses are bad and inferior. Parental approval and the security of bonded love are withdrawn from little boys who persist in exposing their feelings or display so-called effeminate traits.

Youngsters have a difficult time admitting to and coping with jealousy. In order to deal with envy boys develop an explanation for their constricted emotional lives. Feelings are gradually denied, buried, and eventually relegated to "silly" girls. As a cover-up for jealousy boys taunt and demean girls. Girls do not understand that their classmates are jealous of their emotional freedom. They retaliate against the boys by devising their own taunts. The boys-against-the-girls stance lasts until the romantic and sexual urges of adolescence draw the sexes together.

Aggressiveness is the one avenue through which boys may express themselves. Because their other emotions must be held back, the one avenue of expression presents itself in an exaggerated manner. Boys are thought of as normally noisier, quick to fight, physically more active and with shorter attention spans than girls. They *are* more aggressive, but only because of the repressions placed on their other feelings.

Because human experimentation is impossible we can only assume that if female feelings were as restricted as male emotions, girls would display as much aggression as boys. As it is, female aggression appears milder because it is only one of many emotional facets which enjoy expression.

Since aggressiveness is considered appropriate for boys, they become protective and defensive about this male-labeled trait. They do not want girls to invade their one territory of expression. This attitude can carry over into adult life when men are threatened by aggressive women, defining them as unfeminine if they enjoy competition and assertiveness.

The pre-adolescent boy has had several years of training to control his feminine-labeled feelings. He develops workable defenses against them—avoiding play with "repulsive" girls, developing pride in his ability to control tears, convincing himself that boys are the superior sex, teasing female classmates as they shoot ahead in physical and emotional development, and limiting interests to masculine hobbies.

When the eruption of new and insistent feelings occurs in early adolescence, boys are confronted with a psychological dilemma. Their programming clearly states that feelings, except aggression, are inherently female characteristics. Suddenly, they are bombarded by new feelings which clamor for attention and release. Boys' sudden sensitiveness to parental and friends' comments—critical or teasing—cause them to feel tearful, clashing with previous training that boys are not supposed to cry. Preoccupation and fascination with body changes are supposed to be of interest only to "vain" females. Sudden attractions and crushes on girls, male heroes, and women make the young person feel romantic, going against the independent-from-sentiment masculine image.

The youngster struggles to repress the upsurge in emotions but childhood defenses against feelings no longer adequately control the deluge. The cheerful juvenile can quickly become an irritated, quick-tempered, early-adolescent.

The impulsive behavior often seen in this age group is the result of the breakdown of faltering defenses. Of course, girls often act impulsively too, but not with the same degree of aggression which is apparent in boys, who are known for slamming others around, punching, hollering, and sudden acts of mischief.

A boy may be quietly walking down the hall in school and before he knows what has happened he has pulled the fire alarm bell and caused pandemonium in the school. If caught and confronted he will be as surprised as his teachers about his impulsive act. If not apprehended he will feel exhilarated to cause as much external confusion as he feels internally.

"Everything bothers me and makes me mad," said thirteen-year-old John. "I wake up in the morning and feel mean before anything has even happened. I used to help my parents get my little brother and sister ready for school. Now I just want to punch them for acting like babies. When my dad yells at me I feel like exploding but pretend I don't hear him, run to my room and cry into my pillow. I cry a lot and am ashamed to let anyone know. My mom irritates me when she asks what's wrong with me. I can't tell her because I don't know. I only feel right when I'm playing football or basketball with my friends. Wrestling feels good too, but sometimes I get an erection and think I must be queer. I space out on television when I can't stand myself. I like Mork from Ork because he has a good excuse for being confused."

John, like many early adolescent boys, feels alarmed by his constant anger, embarrassed by spontaneous feelings of vulnerability which make him burst into tears, and bewildered by his agitation when his concerned mother questions his state of unhappiness. He attempts to let off excess energies by increased physical activity, but even that does not always bring relief, as he sometimes experiences erections in close contact sports—a normal occurrence, but upsetting to the naive youngster. He blanks out his feelings with the hypnotic, nondemanding television set, identifying with Mork, an alien being who is constantly amazed by human inconsistencies.

Other boys react to the upsurge in feelings by withdrawal, shyness, or compulsive behavior.

"When our fourteen-year-old, Sam, began his adolescence, he became addicted to Chess. He lost interest in his great love, basketball, in his trombone, and school work. He acted as if he had no body—forgot to shower, didn't notice if he wore the same clothes all week, and ate on the run. He constantly read books on Chess, found friends who shared his interest (had several games going simultaneously, plus two Chess through-the-mail games), and moved into a world of moves, strategy and the peculiarities of the Chess pieces. The only time he showed any enthusiasm was when he learned a new move in the game.

"Sam had always been an out-going, athletic child and his sudden switch to an intellectual Chess player was a big surprise to our family. We couldn't get him to join in our activities anymore—bowling, hiking, and skiing.

"Sam was my first experience with a teenager. From my readings I had expected he would be critical, impatient, and rebellious. Instead he was practically oblivious to his father and me. We talked to our pediatrician who advised us not to worry about his compulsive interest. She said it was Sam's way of dealing with the upsurge of instinctual feelings which accompany puberty. She said that his absorption with Chess was harmless and that it probably gave him a sense of control. He was ignoring his physical and emotional changes and concentrating on a mind activity. Her advice to leave him alone and stop trying to fit him into the mold of expected teenage behavior helped me live with Sam's exclusive preoccupation.

"After six months, he dropped Chess as 'silly' and became just as involved with model boat construction. That addiction lasted for two months, then he abruptly gave away all his models to his younger sister. As if he had come out of hermitage, he rejoined the family. The flight into interests which gave him a sense of control seemed to have helped him over the first period of adolescent awkwardness. He was more confident.

"People often say that teenagers are sudden strangers in the house. I think they may act strange sometimes, but they are not strangers. They are the same person but busy adding new parts to themselves. If Sam had to become a game-playing mole or a reclusive model-builder for a time, it seemed to ease his strains, which is the most important thing to me. He emerged as a miniature version of a self-sufficient teenager. During the time he absented himself I had the chance to realize he was becoming independent from us. When he moved into closer involvements with friends and dates, the break from the family didn't seem like such a shock."

Each child will react differently to the increase in feelings as he reorganizes and strengthens his defenses in order to avoid feeling overwhelmed by the onslaught of sensitive reactions. Understanding the jolt which accompanies the onrush of feelings can assist parents when their son may have temper outbursts, become a shy and blushing person, or withdraw into compulsive activities.

In casual conversations parents can explain that it is normal for all teenagers to feel increased sensitivity, romantic and sexual longings, gentleness, anger, and vague sadnesses. This gives a young boy approval, telling him that his feelings do not have to be denied, nor is he less masculine for having them. Sometimes, just the comment that it's okay for teenage boys to cry because they have lots of beginning grown-up feelings can be a great relief to a confused adolescent.

Parents need not feel they have caused damage to boys if they discouraged the expression of "soft" feelings during childhood. The adolescent years are a time of reorganization, growth, and expansion of the personality. Encouraging the acceptance of all feelings will be perceived as part of growing up to be an emotionally balanced adult. Parental approval, discussion, and acceptance will help boys judge the external pressures that continually reinforce the masculine image as aggressive, rather than a combination of all feelings.

"Our family is very emotional," states Mrs. Mias, "and our boys were never discouraged from crying or being tender. They complained that they lived in a compartmentized world. At school they had to pretend to be non-feeling and could only be themselves at home. They didn't like covering up their feelings, but at the same time wanted to be like everyone else. My husband told them that he lived that way too when he was a young man, but doesn't care anymore if other people think he's soft.

"They countered that it was easy for him not to care since nobody is going to criticize a six-foot, two-hundred-pound man. He told them they would have something in life to look forward to and that expecting the world to be fair and caring was a dream. Their dad's honesty about the realities of the world helped the boys to accept their segregated-feeling life, even though they still complain about it and look forward to being 'big enough not to care what people think.'"

Peer Pressures

The majority of your son's peers will most likely never discuss their reactions to their sexual, tender, and sensitive feelings. They will probably deny their insecurities with elaborate rules of conduct in order to prove their masculinity. The self-imposed disciplinary tool inside the youthful group structure is the fear of attracting negative taunts by exposing any "feminine" attitudes.

A successful music major in college told us that his interest in music was halted because of peer pressure in junior high school. He had learned to play the flute in grade school. When he first chose his instrument, some classmates teased him about playing a "girl's flute" (as if a musical instrument knew who is playing it). The youngster complained to his parents about the taunting. His father gave him a demonstration, playing jazz and classical records with flute solo passages. After each record, his father read him the name of the soloist, who in each case turned out to be a man. This information armed the fourth grader to silence his attackers effectively. His playing had a special, rich tone and touch, and he was praised by the band director and other teachers during the next three years. His musical gift became a part of his self-esteem system.

When he began junior high school, he was barraged by older boys making fun of his "little case" with disparaging remarks associating his small flute case with his penis size. They dubbed him "the fairy flute blower." He gave up playing the flute as the pressure increased in viciousness and intensity. Fortunately, he had other abilities which helped him feel worthwhile—athletic grace, good friends, and understanding parents. Giving up the flute would have been a big blow if he had only the one accomplishment. He rediscovered his flute in college, but felt he had lost many years of perfecting his talent. Looking back, he said he felt cowardly about having buckled under the pressure, but that daily hassle had just been too great for his thirteen years.

This kind of vicious reaction from adolescent classmates occurs because in these years boys are unsure of their own masculinity—dealing with their own "soft" feelings—and feel threatened when anyone dares to be different.

Most likely, all boys will receive some humiliating peer teasing and rejection for their "soft" traits or small size during the early teenage years. In order to maintain a stoic social image, boys will retaliate with teasing or fight for their masculine honor. They will rarely encourage further ridicule by revealing hurt feelings or crying in public. These reactions are usually expressed at home, disguised as over-sensitiveness to parents' criticisms about personal habits or messy rooms. Parents find it easier to deal with emotional explosions when understanding they are receiving an overflow of feelings stimulated by social pressures.

As boys now begin the fluctuating process of debonding, it adds fuel to their prickly, overloaded emotions. They must handle social and peer pressures about expected masculine behavior and also start moving away from their childhood identity. The frustrations and anger associated with these tasks are often taken out on the mother. Most children of two-parent families begin debonding from their mothers, since she represents childhood dependence.

Boys move away from mother's affection and control, shrugging off affection or becoming deaf to routine requests.

"I've learned to handle this 'hands off' spurt of rejection with a sense of humor," says a mother of four. "I went to kiss my twelve-year-old the other day. I was leaving on a week's business trip and wanted to kiss everyone goodbye. He's bigger than I and when I reached to put my arm around him he pulled away and managed to maneuver my kiss so that it landed on his shoulder blade. I patted him and said, 'Oh, sorry, I forgot. If a mom kisses or hugs her growing son it means he will shrink back into a little boy. Isn't that so?' He laughed and asked how I knew about such things. I told him I'd be more careful next time and said perhaps we should have a goodbye handshake. This seemed very grown up to him. My older son, no longer threatened by my pats and hugs, returns affection easily. It helps me that I can still remember not wanting my mother to get too close when I was thirteen."

This woman learned not to take personal affront over normal teenage distancing. Her confidence and ability to joke about the matter eased the situation, didn't evoke guilt in her son, and left everyone feeling good.

Young teenagers may be unable to verbalize why they feel irritable, stand-offish, or super-sensitive. Getting them in touch with their feelings can be done by discussing the normal balancing of all feelings during the growing years. A conversation about the ups and downs of emotions can occur when watching a television program which stimulates discussion, while driving together, and when working or playing. As long as the teenager doesn't feel he is receiving a lecture, he will usually be open to listening. This is the time to begin back and forth conversations which set the stage for further and future adult-type discussions. The pre-adolescent child hears directions, commands, and countless instructions from his parents. The young adolescent feels he has moved a step up in dignity when parents talk with, instead of at, him.

As with girls, even if boys receive information about sex in health classes, they are often misinformed, believing tales from friends or thinking that the inviting, voluptuous women displayed in girlie magazines will materialize when they begin dating. When parents feel comfortable discussing sexual matters, boys can learn that their increased sexual urges are natural.

Masturbation increases in early adolescence, fueled by frequent erections and the need to release sexual feelings. Sometimes, masturbation is used to disfuse anxieties caused by frustrations and confusions about fitting in, coping with awkward limbs, and vague fears of being crazy.

Many youngsters experience some guilt about masturbatory fantasies. Psychologically speaking, fantasies differ from daydreams. A daydreamer consciously controls his visual adventure—elaborating scenes of success, creatively building imaginary conquests in athletics, career achievements, and love. A fantasy usually occurs without conscious control, springing from the instinctual well of our more primitive psyches.

A conservative, polite boy may have a fantasy of machine-gunning down all his authority figures in one grand sweep and surprise himself with the intensity of his murderous impulses. In a daydream, the same person might imagine over-shadowing his boring teachers and lecturing parents by winning a debate with brilliant arguments.

Fantasies, similar to the young person's impulsive acts of mischief, are another area over which he seems to have little control. A boy may feel guilty about his sexual and aggressive fantasies if he thinks he has too many or if they are too lurid. Since fantasies are a safety valve which allows excessive feelings an escape, teenagers should understand that they are normal. If you recount your own fantasies with them, they can feel less weird about their own visual images.

Sometimes, boys feel more at ease discussing sexual matters with their father or older siblings. They may feel embarrassed to talk about sex with mothers, since many children think older women are asexual. They may become suddenly modest about being naked, and quickly cover up when mothers walk in when they are dressing. They may blush when sex is mentioned in the presence of mothers. If feeling strange about increased sexual ruminations, boys may avoid looking older women in the eyes, fearing their thoughts may shine through.

Experienced mothers knock before entering teenagers' bedrooms, respect their need for bathroom privacy, and generally maintain a casual approach, ignoring blushing and embarrassed giggling about sex.

As the early adolescent gradually incorporates his new feelings and strengthens his self-image as an independent teenager, he will relax and drop his porcupine-like behavior with his mother. The more accepting she is as he removes himself from her affection, the easier it will be for him to overcome his fear of falling back into "little boy" behavior.

During the phase of debonding from mother, boys normally seek a closer relationship with their fathers as they begin solidifying their masculine image. Single mothers report an upsurge in their sons' hero worship of athletes, coaches, or teachers.

The early adolescent boy, in the service of debonding, gives up a mother's affection to a great extent, and has little chance for mutual touching with girls, but he still retains the need for the comfort of touch. Fathers at ease with their own feelings share more pats, hugs, and kisses with their young sons.

"I have always been a touch-type person, because my family was always hugging and kissing. I *want* to hug and kiss my boys so they don't feel strange about showing good feelings with their friends. They say there's a taboo against boys hugging, except when victorious over athletic achievements. I explained the touch taboo is the macho fear of homosexuality. They conform to the unwritten, no-touch rule now, but I know my affection with them and my own male friends will sink in as natural behavior. I feel sorry for men who can only express friendship love by wrestling or punching."

A father who felt shy about showing overt physical affection for his young teenagers said, "I spent a lot of time doing physical things with them. We play basketball, baseball, and hockey together. I also taught them how to sew and to cook. We talk about life when we are playing and working and I share my love feelings this way. They seem happy with my kind of affection and don't hesitate to talk to me about drugs, girls, and the general dissatisfactions of being young. The main message I want to get across to them is that I value them as special people. I think I'm doing just that."

Both fathers, with their different approaches, satisfy the young teenager's need for masculine attention.

Because athletes are so revered in our society, boys emulate them and compete for places on their school teams. The enjoyment of sports gives youngsters a sense of accomplishment, particularly if they are having a difficult time being industrious students, not uncommon when children are trying to sort out the distracting emotions during this time. The pleasure of playing well and the satisfaction of doing one's best can be a goal in itself. Boys can gain self-confidence from sports activities if parents do not place too much emphasis on winning or always being first. The cultural "first place" mentality causes many fledgling athletes to give up in failure, rather than learning the enjoyment of using one's body.

An excellent tennis player gave up playing when he was sixteen because he felt that all the pleasure had been taken out of the game. He said his parents had pushed him to play in competitions since he was ten. "They wanted me to be a champion, but I just wanted to enjoy the sport. I gave in and played for teams, but knew that when I got big enough I would quit. Why can't parents leave kids alone?" If these parents had let him have fun instead of insisting on playing to win, he might still find tennis a pleasant game.

Physical Changes

Physical maturational signs include muscle and skeletal growth, an increase in the size of the testes with a roughening and reddening of the scrotal skin, followed by growth in the width and length of the penis, the appearance of facial and body hair, and a deepening of the voice.

Boys vary tremendously in physical development, some reaching full physical maturity at fifteen, while others do not complete their growth until twenty. The precocious boy usually does not suffer peer teasing when he shoots ahead of his classmates. He is admired because he can display the superior physical strength associated with masculinity.

Most boys seem impatient to grow tall and muscular, hating it if they lag behind their friends.

A mother told of discovering her slightly built, fourteen-year-old, vehemently studying books on karate, sending forth strange screams and grunts from his bedroom. He said he was tired of being pushed around and planned to pummel bullies at school with self-defense techniques. "He was a year younger than his classmates, plus both sides of our family don't grow until fifteen or sixteen. He disbelieved that he would ever be tall.

"He studied his books and joined a weight-lifting class after school. His muscles expanded but not his height. We sympathized with his plight, but couldn't get too serious as he muttered and complained. Happily, the next year he grew a foot, celebrating every purchase of new pants to fit his longer legs. He's tall now and feels wonderful because he doesn't have to feel like a coward anymore. During his year of tribulation my husband and I bemoaned the emphasis on height equated with personal value but could not convince our son he was a fine person, short or tall. The need to be like everyone else superceded our opinion."

Slow starters worry that they will be forever short. Since bigness is associated with masculine power, a boy who hasn't begun his growth may feel inadequate. He needs emotional support from parents, even if he pretends to ignore love and acceptance. During a routine physical exam, a doctor can explain that the slow starter will soon catch up with his friends. The reassurance from a professional can carry more weight than parental promises, because doctors convey objectivity and a matter-of-fact certainty about growth. Usually, when skeletal growth begins, its quickness and speed equally amazes parents and child.

Many boys do not grow into the tall, muscular ideal of the masculine hero. Adults know physical stature has nothing to do with inner self-esteem or a person's worth. Teenagers learn these values when parents talk about personality traits that are more valuable than height and muscle strength. Praise and appreciation for a short person's other traits—intelligence, creativity, sense of humor—will help him overcome the disappointment of being shorter than his dreams.

"I was always little," says a nineteen-year-old young man, "but I knew some magical day I would be six-foot-two, like my dad. He always told me I would be as tall as him. I'm built like my mother's side of the family. I'm five–nine and it seems like I've stopped growing. I wish my father hadn't promised me I'd be tall, as if it were so important. My girlfriends never complained, so I finally stopped thinking being tall was a necessity for feeling good about my body. By the way, when you write your book could you talk about boys' preoccupation with penis size?"

A great locker room sport has always been heckling and making fun of each other's penis size, everyone pointing to others, hoping their own genitals will escape detection.

Many men confide they still compare themselves to others, saying,

"It's an old habit, hard to break. I still feel inhibited urinating with strangers in public bathrooms, sensing they are negatively judging my penis."

It is extremely difficult to convince boys that a large penis does not bring automatic sexual grace, power over women, or in any way add to one's overall success in life. This fact of life is hopefully learned as they mature and understand women are more interested in gentleness and consideration rather than the length and breadth of penises.

One Foot In, One Out

A boy in early adolescence presents a picture of confusion: a gangly youth, with one precarious foot in the molasses of childhood, struggling to place the other weighted, outstretched foot on some firm ground. Unseen by the youth, the ground he searches for is even more unstable than what he is floundering in now. For the next step toward maturity is the most unsettling of all—the mid-adolescent years.

FOUR

The Mid-Adolescent Years

The majority of high school students can be classified as mid-adolescent youth. These few years before graduating into the "real" world of work, college, or marriage require many social, physical, and emotional adaptations for teenagers as well as parents. Adults have the responsibility of preparing youth for their future and, at the same time, for being attentive to their developing personalities.

Pulling Away from Parents

As we discussed in the chapters on male and female early adolescence, both sexes begin their quest for independence by first debonding from the mother. A boy's need to disconnect in order to define his masculinity appears to be more urgent. Usually, the girl moves away from her mother's domination more slowly, simultaneously seeking validation from her father.

Many women have complained about feeling rejected and used during this shift period. "The children use me only as a chauffeur, a banker, a cook, and a cleanup servant," state mothers, the first targets of debonding.

This urge to distance from mothers can be better accepted if women recognize that they symbolize the childhood dependence which teenagers feel driven to escape and put behind them. This distancing is not a hostile act, but a necessary requirement in their gradual search for individuation.

Great numbers of women we have spoken with enjoy their children's move toward independence, gladly shedding the parental controlling hat they wore during the juvenile years. "It's wonderful to participate in a teenager's desire to free the ties that bind," states Joanne, a mother of one high school daughter.

"I began teaching Sarah independence when she was very young, using a game I invented called, Wants and Jobs. We played it on a blackboard, drawing a chalk line down the middle with the titles of Wants and Jobs. I explained that if she wanted something enough, she could figure out a Job to do in order to gain her Want. I was showing her how actions bring results. At first, because of her age, her Wants were simple and it was easy to figure out a Job. As she became more responsible in junior high school, the game became more complex. Now she uses the Wants and Jobs principle to sort out plans, make decisions and budget her time and money. She uses her father and me as a sounding board rather than the first and last word in decision making.

"She wanted to buy a car and had saved a thousand dollars from grandparents' gifts, a savings account, and her salary from the local supermarket. She also had ambitions to be a cheerleader, but had to weigh the loss of income over the fun and attention of being a cheerleader. The practice time would force her to give up her part-time job.

"My husband said, 'You can always buy a car, but you only have one chance to be a high school celebrity.' I said, 'I think I'd rather have a car than dance and yell in front of a crowd.' We usually differ in our opinions, but Sarah is accustomed to hearing opposite views.

"She decided to train for a cheerleader's position and 'be frivolous while I still have the chance.' Her decision was based on reviewing the pros and cons of car ownership and the carefreeness of being a cheerleader. Because we didn't advise, but rather gave our opinions, Sarah felt her decision was her own. Every choice she makes adds to her growing sense of adulthood. Since I set out to encourage her to think independently, I can't imagine feeling hostile that she uses her own mind and actually doesn't need my directions anymore."

Most early teenagers will admit that they still want mom around, as an anchor of security, but not as the old protector and provider they knew in their recent past.

"Through trial and error with my older teenagers I've learned to expect my high-school son's vacillations, from total independence one day to dipping back into occasional childhood behavior. His brother and sister, in their late twenties, keep telling him he has an easier time than they did. They called me 'Anxious Anna,' 'Worried Wendy,' and 'Invasive Ida' when they were teenagers. I'm such a different person today that Todd doesn't know what they are talking about.

"He has the normal ambivalence about being a young adult which sometimes is revealed in touching ways. He cooks his breakfast and makes a lunch, proud of his ability to take care of himself. The other morning he sheepishly asked if I would make him 'peanut butter toast trains,' a favorite breakfast food when he was little. As I was cutting up the toast he leaned his shoulder into mine and said, 'I just had a funny craving to feel like a goofy kid again, slurping up mom's toast trains.' He enjoyed his brief feeling of being served toast trains and quickly reverted to his 'in-charge' personality as he put his lunch together."

A mother of an independent fifteen-year-old daughter gave a good example of being temporarily needed. Her daughter, suffering from delusions caused by a high fever, woke her up in the middle of the night. The girl was crying and whimpering about the pins sticking in all her pores and the thousands of small, pointed rocks being thrown at her. The fever-related delusion made the girl feel helpless, afraid, and "like a little baby again." When people experience delusions they have real reactions and feelings; they become panicked. The mother quickly put her arm around her tall daughter, murmured reassuring words, and steered her into a cool shower to bring the fever down. She then dried her off, gave her two aspirins, and tucked her back into bed, comforting the frightened youngster. As the fever subsided, so did the hallucinations and the fears.

In the morning, the fever was gone and the girl was back to her normal, somewhat distant, teenage self. The mother confided that although the incident had been mildly alarming, "It felt good to be totally needed once again." At the moment of the daughter's panic, the youngster had needed an all-caring mother. But the mother had enough experience with two older adolescents to refrain from baby-ing her daughter once she was feeling healthy again.

Teenagers are not grateful when parents act wisely—when parents know whether to give emotional support or to hold back. The satis-faction of wise action has to come from the parents' own joy in know-ing they are doing the right thing.

"I was delighted to give up the position of the controlling mother when my teenagers began straining against the reins. It took some time to realize they needed the freedom to choose—Should I study or goof off? Is this friend loyal or using me? Can I stay up all night and still play good team tennis tomorrow? Can I avoid showers and still be acceptable?—the early personal decisions of life management which I had always overseen. I didn't interfere by voicing my concerns when they chose to indulge themselves.

"My daughter had easily maintained an A average until high school. Her second semester card had three Cs. She was amazed and expected me to be angry. I told her that it was her report card, not mine. Normally, I have found teenagers look for someone else to blame, rather than admitting their own mistakes. I think they use this protective defense because they think admission of mistakes will crumble their shaky self-esteem system.

"She rambled on about teachers disliking her as an excuse for her average grades. After her long-winded explanation ran out, she finally owned up to avoiding homework, hoping to coast through. She then turned to me, accusing me of not forcing her to study. I asked her if she really wanted to be monitored like an irresponsible child. We talked about successful self-determination—do your work, earn an A, goof off and earn a C. Throughout the conversation I maintained a stance of a helpful guide rather than soothing, sympathizing, or falling back into the all-knowing mother. I could have told her she made the wrong choice, coasting instead of applying herself. If I had jumped on her she would have been reduced to the 'bad' student who needed parental reprimanding. By letting her discover her own errors, she could take responsibility for her own actions.

"It's exhilarating to watch a teenager move from surprise at the results of poor planning, blaming external forces, demanding the parent share the blame, and then looking at their own mistakes. My motto is relax, be patient, and let teenagers make some blunders. This approach has taught me to keep silent when I would have liked to remind and direct. When my teenagers are adults I hope to tell them how hard it was for me to patiently hold back my opinions. At the present I don't expect accolades."

Shirley, a mother of one teenager, states, "My mother tried every guilt maneuver to keep me childish. She acted as if I were a traitor when I wanted to be with my friends instead of spending time with her. She even said I was sticking a knife in a mother's heart. Her ploys worked most of the time. I felt miserably pulled between my social life and her demands for me to ease her loneliness. My father was one of those stereotyped high-powered businessmen who had little time for his family. She was passive and refused to make her own life, using me as a companion.

"I vowed then I would never use guilt to manipulate my children. When Barbara was young, I discovered that I used more subtle forms to induce guilt in my child. I was never as obvious as my mother, but I was getting similar results—an angry child, complying in order to avoid the crushing feeling of guilt. I was horrified that I had unconsciously identified with my mother's tactics. I went into psychotherapy for my sake and my daughter's too. I wanted to exorcise that part of me that was repeating old family patterns. Making children feel guilty in order to control their lives is using an unfair power—if you don't do what I want, I'll suffer and you'll be sorry.

"I enjoy my daughter's company. She's a delightful person. Her boyfriend thinks so, too, and they spend the majority of their free time together. I wouldn't dream of demanding she spend time with me, unless she wanted to. My sensitivity to invasion of teenage freedom by parental pressure pushed me to extreme behavior, never suggesting we do mother-daughter things. The other day she said, 'Why don't we ever have lunch and go shopping on Saturdays like Denise and her mom?'

"She has no idea how hard I have worked to give up being a guilt manipulator. She enjoys freedom as a result of my therapy. My pride in overcoming my identification with my neurotic mother greatly satisfies me. I don't expect Barbara to appreciate my efforts. I'm just glad to know I could break up unhealthy child-rearing patterns."

Mid-adolescents who experience debonding with their mother's acceptance and approval become friendlier during high school. They feel their need to separate has been encouraged and are not as jumpy about seeking advice, or fearful that their mother will treat them like a little child. They take parental maturity in stride, unaware that you may have worked hard to let them go. Mothers may feel jealous because her children, particularly boys, maintain a close bond with the father while ignoring her. "After all I've done for you!" Remembering that this move away from mother is essential can help with envious feelings while a woman is slowly, or sometimes suddenly, eased out of the tightly knit mother-child bond. This period is an opportunity for the mother to change energy directions and develop new skills for personal self-esteem.

Over half the female population has joined the work force. The increased involvement with a job, and its energy and time demands, often automatically reduces reactions to debonding—too busy to feel left out. Intense reactions of feeling pushed aside may surface if you are a homemaker who has devoted the majority of your emotional energies to raising children. The self-esteem achieved from bonded mothering can be replaced with pride in letting go, investigating talents which inject new interest in life, or volunteering mothering skills to needy causes.

One mother told us that after her teenagers confronted her with the label of "an overprotector," she realized that she was reminding them of their childhood years, clucking over their routines, and still treating them as forgetful children. "When I was forced to give up my super-mom attitude, I was amazed at how much psychological and physical energy I had left for myself," she said.

At this point in her children's lives, the mother's job is far from complete, but it is the time when early and middle teenagers are driven to separate their childish attachment and own up to their emerging adultness. A self-assured mother need not take this "arm's length" distancing as rejection but, instead, accept it as a positive sign of growth.

Many mothers have discussed with us an interesting inner occurrence which sometimes coincides with teenage debonding. They have noticed a sudden drop or gradual disappearance of their mothering instincts. One woman described her feelings: "I noticed that I stopped having that old 'heart in the throat' clutching response when the kids were hurt or upset. I didn't love them any less, I just didn't feel all that motherly. I felt more like an interested friend. At first I felt guilty, since this motherly feeling had been a big part of my character for twenty years. At the same time, my husband seemed to become more involved with the problems of our teenagers, while I felt kind of bored with their dramatic intrigues. We talked about our feelings and decided that perhaps, in our case, my mothering pool dried up when my teenagers were ready to leave my side, and my husband's fathering pool was stimulated as our teenagers became more adult."

This mother also said that for years she had been preparing children to be responsible, active, problem-solvers, and independent people. "Now that they are ready, I'm interested in their productions, whether in school, creative pursuits, or love choices. My husband wants to be the helping parent now and that's great with me, but I have some complaints.

"I didn't consider him to be a good father when our children were small. In fairness, he had never wanted children, finding them boring. I insisted on parenthood and ended up doing the majority of parenting for our two girls. He was a disciplinarian, never played with them, and vocalized resentment about all the time I spent with them. Now, I feel he's getting the benefits of all my labors. He's just as surprised that he likes teenagers, and they don't hold a grudge that he virtually ignored them before—they probably think it's all normal. We talk about the disparities in our parenting feelings, which helps clear the air. Our girls listen in and think we're 'weird, but the only parents they have.'"

Another mother said she also experienced an evaporation of motherliness. "The problem was that I had raised three children and still had an eleven-year-old son. I found myself telling him, 'I'm too old to deal with going to school if you misbehave. You'll just have to learn to deal with teachers by yourself.' I would have been amazed at myself if I had felt this disinterest with my first child. The consequence of my backing off as the normal, concerned mother is that my last child matured much faster than the first who had the old 'hovering' mom to take care of things."

Debonding, then, can also occur in parents. Since humans are not mechanical, the process is not always simultaneous, but parents and their children seem to manage with surprising resiliency.

During these years, the father must adjust as both sons and daughters pull away. His wife, who has experienced this seeming rejection first, can be a helpmate if her husband has difficulties letting go graciously. He may have a more perplexing time accepting the dethronement from his daughter than from his son. Her adoration and affection have usually been more obvious than a son's idealization of his dad.

As nature instinctively nudges teenagers away from parental ties, young people are entering into the unknown. They are searching for their own separate selves, unique ethical and value systems, and future life commitments. They are leaving behind the safety of childhood. While they are divesting themselves of their bonds with the past, they unconsciously mourn giving up the pleasant haven of the parental umbrella of bondedness. Mourning involves sadness, irritability, anger, depression, and a final acceptance of loss. Adolescent mourning of lost childhood is unique because no concrete loss seems evident; however, the loss is very real.

The teenagers' journey through mourning into the rebirth of distinct identities is eased when parents understand the process of normal mourning. Teenagers are unaware that a part of them longs and grieves for the carefree days of childhood. It does them little good to be told that they are in a temporary state of mourning. Parents can help by simply understanding another source of their adolescents' sudden emotional vacillations, outbursts of anger, bouts of depression, and sullen withdrawal from family activities.

Parents also mourn the passage of their children's childhood, but they should try to avoid manipulations that unconsciously call teenagers back to childlike ways. Wise parents hold back saying, "But you always loved going to the lake (movies, grandma's, restaurant) with us!" or "You were always such a cheerful child; what's wrong with you?" or "I liked you better when you did what you were told." These guilt-inducing statements produce the impression that the small, non-opinionated, easily controlled child is preferred to the changing teenager. If you feel like mourning the simpler days of child-rearing, do so with mates or friends, out of hearing of sensitive adolescents.

Concurrently, the obvious physical and sexual growth of teenagers can cause mourning in adults. As parents are confronted with the limitations of careers, the beginning of physical decline, and the signs of aging, they experience the loss of their own youth as their children surge ahead with vigor and vitality. These feelings are further deepened as teenagers devalue parental life style and once-admired traits, and abandon the adoration based on childhood bonds.

Teenagers talk about parents' possessions, activities, and interests as "old": "this *old* house," "this *old* car," "the same *old* food," "those *old* friends." We *are* old to them, just as we have always been. The difference is that adolescents are compelled to verbalize the distinction between their youth and our age in order to separate themselves further from us. For this reason teenagers suffer acute embarrassment if parents try to act youthful by intruding on peer conversations or usurping the special language of youth.

"My mother can't face the fact that she's old," says an angry daughter. "She's thirty-seven and still wants to have guys flirt with her. That's okay, I guess, but I wish she'd leave my boyfriends alone. We were all sitting around the pool the other day, and she came out in a string bikini! I thought I'd die. She actually had the nerve to flirt with *my* boyfriend. She's better at it than me, so the next thing I know, they're swimming together."

The mother doesn't consider herself old and wants to feel attractive. She is being unfair, however, to compete with her daughter for the young boy's approval. Teenagers feel that parents already have had their turn at youth and resent parents who try to be one of the gang.

Adults do not have to be defined by their adolescents' view of them. Life is an opportunity for endless personal possibilities. When our children begin to turn away from us, our attentions can be directed toward many other things: establishing preventive health habits; learning to be more intimate and joyful with our life-mates; developing talents long neglected because of childcare duties; and enjoying life to its fullest. Adults can replace the pleasure of being admired by all-accepting children with personal self-appreciation for their own growth and with freedom to explore new avenues of creativity.

Conflicting Emotions, Unfinished Personalities

The middle-adolescent person (and he or she is vehement about being treated as a person—not as a "kid" or "child") is beset with conflicting emotions that cause mood swings or vacillations in emotional reactions. These contradictions in behavior can occur inside of an hour or a day. As the pendulum swings from exhilaration to despair, mood alterations make teenagers appear to be mixed up in their approach to and feelings about parents, siblings, and friends. A teenager's emotional life is filled with ambivalence—conflicting feelings about self and others. Most of these ups and downs focus on the parents, from whom teenagers are trying to disconnect. The majority of rebellious acts and statements are simply disguised forms of breaking away from dependency ties with the parents, rather than true, personal attacks on them.

Adults who sincerely desire their children's maturity and independence understand these debonding maneuvers and take them in stride. Buffered by a healthy sense of humor, they can survive with ease many of the more transparent attempts to disconnect.

The most obvious external signs of distancing from the past generation are changing dress and hair styles to conform to the peer fashion rather than parents' ideas of what teenagers should look like. Making an issue about dress and hairstyles is a losing battle. Centering the need to control teenagers around their appearance is a waste of everyone's energies. Adolescents are extremely sensitive about their personal statements via dress and hairstyles—to themselves and to each other. They don't care what style parents think appropriate.

"My father is always telling me to get a haircut," says Jody. "I finally told him my girlfriend loves my hair the way it is. I asked him if I should wear it to please him or her. It's the first time I ever won a point with him."

Other teenagers complain that they feel their privacy invaded when parents criticize their clothes or hair. "The more my mother frets and urges me to get my hair cut and wear 'decent' clothes, the more I want to stand up for myself," says a girl with a wild, frizzy mop and a gypsy outfit.

Strange or unusual outfits or hairdos are a badge of independence from parents who have always controlled choices. When adults tease and make fun of teenagers' styles, they are demeaning the entire person—that's the way an adolescent feels.

If a person thinks he or she looks great and friends agree, parents should be silent or complimentary. Believe it or not, the "wild" teenager will really look acceptable some day.

In mid-adolescence, both sexes are concerned and preoccupied with their body image, comparing themselves to heroes, and wanting to appear casually unconcerned about their physical attributes. However, they spend many hours staring into the mirror, minutely inspecting every flaw with a sense of hopelessness.

Teenagers who develop acne are aghast by the eruptions on their faces, sure people turn away from their disfigurement in disgust.

"My friends call me Pizza Face because they say my pimples look like Italian sausage slices. They don't know how awful I feel about my face. I just smile like everything's fine, but inside I am a walking, talking bug." Tony shared his feeling with his sympathetic father who makes sure Tony keeps his appointments with the dermatologist and gives his son plenty of affectionate attention. Tony wants to hide his head under a hood. His friends are probably not intentionally cruel, just unthinking. The support he receives from his father helps, but cannot completely soothe his distorted self-image and the resultant social inhibitions he feels.

Even one or two pimples can make a self-conscious teenager feel like a freak. Peoples' view of themselves revolves around their facial characteristics—vision, language, olfactory and auditory sensations are experienced through their face and head. Any disturbance causes extreme distress, particularly for the teenager who is continually examining his face.

Daily skin care is essential during these years when enlarged facial pores secrete more oil. The oil combines with dirt and dust, forming blackheads which plug the pores. Ordinary germs get under the blackheads and cause pimples. Nervous teenagers finger, squeeze, and break pimples spreading the germs to other areas.

Cleaning the face and hands twice a day with hot soapy water, rinsing with hot, followed by cold water (to close the pores) can prevent the spread of acne.

In the last few years dermatologists have available to them new, effective ointments, cleaning solutions, and antibiotics. Many of these new products help prevent the scarring which was so prevalent in past generations. They direct their treatment to educating their patients about the use of these medications and do not emphasize giving up sweet and greasy foods, although they ask their young patients to try for moderation.

A colleague of ours relates that he has great sympathy for teenagers who suffer from acne. He insists their parents utilize the services of dermatologists. He still retains the scars from his own youth and remembers, "All my friends and I were covered with ugly pustules, and we pretended not to care. We suffered in silence, staring in disbelief into our mirrors. Our parents said it was just a phase."

While teenagers are undergoing treatment for acne they need extra affection and sympathy from parents. This can be given by engaging the teenager in conversations about his or her opinions, ideas and interests which do not relate to appearances, revealing that the disfigurement does not detract from the person's lovability.

"My legs are too long, but I can handle that as most of my friends are gangly and lurching around, but I can't stand my big nose and the blackheads on it. I feel like that's all people see and hate me for the black spots on my ski-slope nose," complained sixteen-year-old Eric.

His father took him to a hair stylist who treated Eric's problem as an everyday challenge. He said, "Noses should be made more attractive by one's haircut. We'll part your hair in the middle and feather the sides to reduce frontal impact." The illusion created made Eric feel less conspicuous. He learned how to use a complexion brush to keep his pores clean. His father said the expense was worth it, just to get Eric's attention away from feeling ugly. "If he feels more attractive, he'll have more confidence in himself.

"Feeling good about your face is important, just so a person can forget about it and concentrate on more important things. I waited a month for Eric to grow accustomed to his better looks and then joked with him about our family's large noses. I kidded him into realizing that my nose didn't stop his mother from loving me. With typical adolescent candor he asked why she had been attracted to me. It gave me the foot in the door I wanted to talk about personality traits which appeal to women.

"We talked about showing an interest in a girl's feelings and her activities, and trying to be friends by sharing experiences, getting involved together in doing things and letting one's looks be secondary. I try not to lecture about values, but look for ways to work my thoughts into the conversation in a light-hearted way. Kids see and hear that only the most beautiful and handsome are appealing and acceptable. They need to hear about real values from parents." As very few teenagers are beautiful or handsome, they can be shown that attractiveness is not equal to worthiness.

Parents reveal this credo by praising their teenagers' triumphs, even if the victories are small, thanking them when they help out, and validating their kindliness with troubled friends. Thoughtful words of praise sink into the growing person's value system, giving an example of personal worth via personality traits rather than physical superiority.

Many young people understand that physical perfection is a superficial value judgment, and for heroes they choose television or movie actresses or actors who look ordinary but come across as nice people. Although a healthy body and good grooming are attainable through effort, the desire for perfection in looks will only lead to feelings of inferiority. Learning to develop character qualities should be the goal of growing youngsters.

"My sister is gorgeous and people have always gushed over her. It's probably why I can't stand her," reports a high-spirited, ordinary appearing seventeen-year-old senior. "I was so jealous when we were kids because she got so much attention by just being pretty. I refused to compete with her so-called charms—all she did was smile coyly and boys fell all over her. I figured I would need a good personality if I wanted attention. I thought you could learn to be interesting and spiritually attractive—since I didn't have a choice I thought I'd better learn. My mom helped me. She's pretty too, but said she never counted on her looks to help her get through medical school. She said she wanted to be admired for her brains since a mind lasted longer than flawless skin.

"My sister was very popular, but she never grew into a multi-dimensional person. She and her husband seem bored with each other. I find her boring myself.

"Reaching for a good personality makes you forget about your looks because you pay attention to other people's feelings. The best advice my mother gave me was to stop worrying about other people judging me, that they were too busy worrying about themselves to spend a lot of time thinking about me. It kind of knocked off a view that teenagers have that everyone is spending as much time thinking about them as they do themselves. Her advice helped me relax and be comfortable with myself and others. I have lots of friends and dates who choose me because they like *me,* not because I'm pretty."

Parents whose teenagers feel inferior because of their body or facial structures can stimulate self-esteem by praising their emerging adultness and by showing acceptance with verbal and physical affection. When an adolescent continues to complain about the social structure based on looks, parents can promise that when adult relationships form they are based on trust, loyalty, and mutual care much more than looks.

Directing teenagers toward active involvement in sports, clubs, hobby groups, and intellectual achievements for self-esteem, can remove their preoccupation with physical deficiencies. Any consuming interest will entail interaction with others, and the focus turns to group goals rather than self-criticism, directing energies to getting along together and developing personality richness. Even if a teenager is considered attractive, he or she will be obsessed with some other fault, such as, "I'm too selfish (jealous, dumb, or clumsy) to ever be any good in life." Self-esteem grows from learning self-control, developing judgment, experiencing achievements, attaining realistic goals, and being able to maintain friendship and love relationships.

Every time teenagers make a step forward in these growing-up tasks, your compliments infuse gains with importance. When they naturally fail, your emotional support lends them courage to try again. This is a good time to shelve comments about poor posture, nervous gestures, and irritating habits as teenagers denounce themselves regularly.

All information about concrete values, which we hope our children will absorb, does not have to be verbalized to them. They are always listening in to adult conversations and any comments they hear which reinforce common sense over superficial values will be remembered. They may not incorporate these beliefs until long after leaving home, when parental opinions assume a renewed respect. They may even disagree, but only in the service of being different from the "ice-age generation"—a term one of our teenagers recently dubbed our youth.

Self-esteem begins in childhood, grows during the juvenile years, and fluctuates during the highly charged adolescent personality-solidification process. Each person should have many areas from which to draw a feeling of worth.

In a teenage seminar on the psychology of bartering we had students draw up lists of skills which they could use for bartering. They became enthusiastic and proud when we explained that their skills should be thought of as an integral part of their personal worth inventory.

A student mentioned, "We keep forgetting that doing something well means we should use it to feel good. I'm always getting depressed if everyone doesn't like me. I'm working on liking myself because I can be kind, I can perform well in school, I can play a musical instrument and I'm even nice to my little brother!"

Self-esteem based on achievement is a broader base from which to draw strength than the assurance of being attractive. The boy or girl who learns to gain favors or popularity by depending on physical charms never learns to develop and use personality traits which involve sharing, caring, dependability, and trust.

"I was a cute kid," related Jason, "with curly red hair, freckles and a grin to match any Walt Disney moppet. I remember using my tricks—twinkle eyes, dimples, and boyish smile—to con grade-school teachers into being their pet. It helped with grades, too. I was everybody's little darling. No one guessed that I was orchestrating them with my charms. When my looks changed from cute to gruesome I lost my trick to avoid real work. I felt angry and cheated. Why hadn't someone stopped me? I had to start learning to earn my attention from others and it was hard because I had never thought about being generous or sincere. I'm still trying to be more honest and straightforward with people. I wish I'd been plain looking when I was little so I would have learned to get along instead of using my looks to play games with adults."

"I make my living with my face and figure," reported Blair, an attractive woman in her thirties, "but my fashion model career will soon end as I am replaced by younger women. When my daughter was fifteen she complained because she didn't inherit my height and leaness. She felt cheated because she was 'so brainy' instead of beautiful. She thought modeling was the ultimate in glamour. I wanted to tell her how fortunate she was, how I had felt like a skinny giant when I was a teen and she should be grateful for her intelligence. She wouldn't have understood.

"Instead, last summer I took Vicky with me on a hectic shooting schedule for a catalogue layout. She watched me sweat in the heat, modeling fur coats. She saw the make-up people create illusions of perfection obliterating complexion problems that many models develop from wearing heavy make-up. Chatting with my co-workers, she learned that most of them constantly fret about their faces and bodies, always dieting, exercising and giving up late-night parties in order to look fresh in the morning. She witnessed people in charge treating models like clothes hangers.

"The other models kept asking Vicky if she planned to attend college some day. They revere advanced education, as most of them never finished traditional schooling. She was surprised that my glamorous friends would envy her future. At the end of the day, she asked, 'Why do you do it?' 'It supports us, and I don't know how to do anything else.'

"My motivation was to reveal that having a model's figure does not bring glories or adoration, but is only a means to a job—a hard job. Vicky stopped complaining, and even became more considerate when I arrived home late and exhausted from a shooting session."

If you are the rare naturally beautiful or handsome adult whose teenager is homely, he or she does not necessarily have to suffer from inferiority. We are culturally programmed to believe that attractive people do not suffer from low self-esteem, rejection fears, or self-doubts. Good-looking adults know this to be a romantic myth. Parents can confide, and thereby instruct their youngster, that engaging looks are secondary to feeling personal worth, and that people must project inner warmth in order to earn friendship and love.

In our experience, children of celebrities do not feel overshadowed by their parent's superior physical attributes. Their main complaint is the forced parental absences which occur in the entertainment business. In order to avoid their children's feeling inferior in the light of their fame, celebrities often mention that they try to keep their home atmosphere as normal as possible. "Our children understand that the entertainment business is hard work. They don't think of us as the image we project, but just as frustrating parents," is a consensus of famous parents.

A professor and his wife, a novelist, shared their family's history with us. "Three of our four children were precocious, crawling, walking, and talking very early. They all enjoyed school, were creatively mischievious, and extremely verbal. Our fourth son developed normally, appearing slower in contrast to his siblings. He was quiet, easy to manage, and hated every minute of school. Following his brilliant brothers and sisters caused him to feel inferior, since he did not perform as well as they had. He was frustrated until high school when his mechanical talents blossomed. He asked us why he couldn't think and talk like the other kids. We explained that mechanically oriented people think in pictures rather than ideas, but both ways of seeing things were valuable. His adult success in auto mechanics has helped him overcome his feeling of being a 'silent Martian' in a family of non-stop talkers."

Parents need not feel disappointed if their children do not inherit their gifts. A child with average intelligence can be loved and accepted for himself, gaining self-esteem from belonging in a family, rather than his acceptance resting on intellectual achievements.

As mid-teenagers are gradually coming to terms with their biology and sexuality, their past and their future, plus learning to establish love and friendship bonds, we must not judge or brand them. They are unfinished, and it is unfair to evaluate them as complete in character, opinions, or achievements.

"In my opinion, my extremely bright daughter's high school years were a disaster. Her listless attitude produced average grades inconsistent with her intelligence. She said school work was boring. I kept nagging her and insisting she do something constructive with her life. I called her lazy and stupid. In return I received veiled looks of hostility. My name-calling effectively shut me out of her real interest— movie production. She was always going to the movies and reading magazines and books which I thought was a waste of time and never hesitated to say so," reports Bill, an older father.

"If I had it to do over again, I would have paid more attention to what interested her, instead of assuming she should be excited about normal schoolwork. It was as if she was just waiting until graduation from high school in order to enroll in film school. Today, at twenty-two she's a productive, successful film editor, loving her work and the creative people she deals with. All my name calling was for naught. I thought she was going to be a useless blob forever, but I was completely wrong. She's kind enough not to remind me of those unhappy years when I badgered her."

"My parents kept telling me I was selfish and inconsiderate," says a mother of three teenagers, "and their label has stuck with me throughout life. Whenever I choose to do something just for myself, I hear an inner voice saying, 'You always think of your selfish interests first.' My folks had no idea that self-centeredness is analagous to adolescence. They also believed children's good character traits formed with criticism and that commendations guaranteed swollen egos.

"My children have many faults but I try to resist calling them names associated with their flaws. I know a teenager feels 'all dumb,' 'all awkward,' or 'all inconsiderate' when branded with those humiliating personality tags. I've made a concentrated effort to say, 'I don't like that part of you which keeps ignoring requests, bullies your little brother, or forgets others need the phone.' I want them to feel they have specific irritating habits, not that their total person is unlikable. I also believe that they require compliments in order to balance the internal and external criticisms they hear. All teenagers have some good qualities. Sometimes, a parent just has to look hard to find them. I'd rather search out and mention their lovable traits than harp on their faults."

Our expectations, hopes, and dreams for evolving teenagers must be tempered with a realistic view of the times and the limitations of their own uniqueness. You cannot predict the kind of a person your teenager will become based on actions during the commotion of adolescence. You need only reread the description of your authors' tumultuous teen years to recognize that classifying young people is risky. You might not be able to reap the rewards of satisfaction for responsible parenting until your children are adults.

Teenagers who hear parents labeling them as irresponsible, not involved enough, lazy, or failures feel thwarted, and bitter about being so judged. Teenagers who are successful feel as squeamish in the face of too much praise as they are unsure about their ability for continued performance. Teenagers are people who are involved with complex internal and external tasks that require parental support, love, guidance, and sympathy. Pointing out faults can be done in many ways besides branding, lecturing, and scolding.

A man who became the homemaker in his family was irritated because his teenagers left their dirty clothes all over the floor. "Their mother had been picking up after them all their lives, so they naturally left dirty clothes where they dropped," he said. "Instead of calling them slobs, I asked them a couple of times to help me out by bringing laundry to a basket by the machine. There was agreement, but no action. I decided that since they didn't care about my request, I wouldn't worry about their clothes. I wasn't going to wash until my basket was full. After three days I started hearing complaints about no socks and underwear. Five days elapsed before all their clothes were dirty. I remained silent as they grumbled and wore the same thing two days in a row—a social disaster in their peer group. Soon they came trooping out with all their rags to be cleaned. I don't have an empty clothes basket anymore."

The same man taught his children to appreciate the food they ate and the efforts of the person who prepared it. He figured that when they grew up and served food to guests or their spouses, they and their mates would want to be praised for their efforts. When they wolfed down their meals without comment, he said he thought he deserved compliments for his efforts. It soon became routine for them to comment on the meals. He explained, "I'm new at serving people. My wife never seemed to mind when children took her work for granted. I mind. Even though I like our switch, with her working and me running the house, I think it's civilized for young people to learn to think about those who provide for them. At first, they thought my tactics were nuts, but there's nothing like dirty clothes and appropriate demands for appreciation to teach living lessons, without name-calling either."

Parental support provides financial and home security and the comfort of adult assurance, as well as an acceptance of the teenager's normal vacillations, contradictions, and ambivalences. Love flows from the parental bond, which allows the stretching and discarding of childhood ties while teenagers search for their personal meaning. Giving affection through physical demonstrations can reveal love—if those hugs, kisses, and pats are dispensed without making teens feel like little kids. Love also means listening to your teenagers when they need an understanding adult. Being unselfish, parental love can be dispensed without expecting too much consideration in the present, for the parent knows that mid-adolescents are naturally self-absorbed. Love lets go.

Giving guidance to the teenager is being confident enough to set family standards and rules, being able to say "no" when teens seek approval for obviously dangerous activities. A guiding parent presents reality to teenagers instead of sugar coating the world in a naive attempt to protect and buffer their sensitivities. Guidance means setting an ethical standard about acceptable behavior inside and outside the family.

The sympathetic parent will empathize with teenagers in their struggle to grapple with, sort out, and make some form of adjustment to their feelings. The hurts, rejections, and failures that teenagers face push them to seek solace in the security of a family's love. Also their victories, loves, and achievements require suitable praise and celebration from the parents.

Teenagers can accept sympathy, emotional support and praise when these encouragements are delivered in a different language from what was used in their childhood.

"My mother used to distract me with food when I was little and unhappy. She knows candy and cookies don't help me now and instead, she's become a great listener," says Shelly, a fifteen-year-old.

"My biggest gripe concerns my girlfriends. They have a really stupid rule. No matter what plans we have made, if a boy asks them out, they automatically cancel 'girl' arrangements. I get furious and call them disloyal and unreliable. They only feel alive if a boy shows interest in them. I want to feel good about myself without judging my worth in terms of a boy's attention.

"When I complained to my mother, she didn't take sides with me against my girlfriends, but tried to understand my feelings and why my friends act so insecure. She said her girlfriends act the same way. We ended up having a long conversation about personal ethics, something I hadn't given much thought to because I was so busy being angry. My mother turned my attention to a larger issue—how self-esteem can be built on an individual ethical system rather than romantic acceptance. I gave a speech about growing a unique moral system during the adolescent years to my psych class. It stimulated my classmates to think and talk about their responsibilities in friendships.

"I like my mother's approach—not sympathetic, but urging me to think of underlying reasons for other people's behavior."

While we strive to be objective, helpful, and encouraging to teen-agers, we must also deal with their necessary devaluation of us as an aspect of debonding. Parents need a great well of self-confidence while managing their parenting tasks during their children's adolescence.

Helping With Career Choices

Our generation revered advanced education. Children of today must realistically weigh and evaluate their career choices, unencum-bered by the myth that a college diploma guarantees career success. Also, many parents who assumed that they would be sending their offspring to college are no longer in a financial position to offer this automatic luxury.

Although education still is a significant factor in commanding a good job, a college degree is no longer a guarantee of employment. Many satisfactory jobs require vocational or specialized education, for example, the job of the auto mechanic, carpenter, secretary, dental or medical technician, electrician, plumber, or welder. Many of these jobs generate salaries between $10,000 and $27,000 a year. Unless a young person feels driven to become a professional, which demands four to fifteen years of advanced education, college is often a baby-sitting institution which keeps young adults protected from the real world.

During high school, students are pressured to make decisions about future careers. We cannot leave the dispensing of career information solely in the hands of educators. Parents can help by exposing their children to people involved in jobs which attract youngsters.

Our community has a sharing plan with businessmen, professionals, craftsmen, and laborers. High-school students become "helpers" for six months, learning the reality of different jobs. Fantasies or miscon-ceptions about glamorous occupations are soon dispensed with as job realities become clear. Several idealistic teenagers who wanted to "help their fellow man" worked in a mental health clinic for six months. At the end of their stint, the comments were as follows:

"I didn't realize how much clients drain the emotions of a therapist."

"The poverty was too much for me to handle."

"I could never be sympathetic toward abusive parents; I just hated them."

"I really loved working with the children."

"We didn't get anything back from the people—like they weren't grateful for our care or time."

In this program, the students had an opportunity to compare the promises of the job with the realities. They could make evaluations from direct on-the-job observations through participation. They also had the opportunity to talk with working adults who shared their feelings of accomplishment and disillusionment.

You can make these opportunities available to your children if your community does not have a similar program of job exposure. Most adults will take the time to explain honestly what their jobs entail. Young people want to hear the pros and cons about everything.

Quite outside any planned program of job education, our community had an eye-opening experience about the glamor of making movies. A production company advertised for hundreds of extras and hired people from ages eleven through seventy. The enthusiasm was soon dampened when the extras discovered that acting is largely a very boring experience. The actors spend 80 percent of their time waiting while the sound, lighting, and stage crews set up their equipment. The performers then act out a portion of a scene, not once, but often twenty times, until the director thinks it is just right. The production company complained because, after several days of filming, many of the young extras quit, even though they were receiving adequate pay and free food. The major reason given for quitting was that people couldn't stand the boredom.

We have a moral obligation to research job interests with high school children, without inflicting our own expectations upon them. They should not be expected to follow the dreams of our own youth, nor should they be promised glories which are realistically unattainable. If children display interest and aptitude for service work, mechanical repair, carpentry, restaurant work, or technical skills, give them the opportunity to learn these jobs, which have as much dignity as any supposed status position.

Because of increased job longevity, with legislation that removed mandatory retirement age, and the decline in the "one job for life" approach, children should be encouraged to explore more than one kind of talent or interest. They should read the "Occupational Outlook Handbook" available in libraries or from the Superintendent of Documents, Government Printing Office, Washington, D.C. 20402. This handbook offers information about future employment opportunities, discussing job locations and salaries, experience and educational requirements, and hard facts about the changing economic structure and how it affects jobs (such as city civil service jobs once thought secure, but now becoming risky as urban fiscal health declines).

Preparing Them for Future Responsibilities

Personal life management skills are honed during high school years, preparing young people for college attendance, joining the work force, or living independently. Teenagers' natural curiosity for experimentation and their push toward individuation help them develop judgment and tools to handle future challenges.

Any opportunity teenagers have to work, travel, and take responsibilities for their own actions will add to their inner resources. These strengths will be used to deal with the normal psychological jolts they will experience when shifting from home to new environments.

"Our children look forward to attending college. They think it will be a haven away from their impinged city life," report the parents of two high school seniors. "Their school is beset with racial tensions and violence. They can't wait to study and live on a quiet campus, away from physical danger—a respite from the 'protect-yourself-at-all-times' mentality of their present situation. The reality of their unsafe school situation has taught them to be alert for their personal safety. Their advanced education will broaden their views, and the combination of survival and intellectual skills should make them into well-rounded adults, able to handle all types of experiences."

"I'm glad my parents encouraged me to take away-from-home summer jobs during high school," reports David, a freshman at the University of Michigan. "I didn't feel homesick like many of the freshmen in my dorm. Being on my own was both exhilarating and confusing. The world of intense intellectual competition here was deflating at first, since I had never been challenged by so many brilliant people. After I adjusted to my low man on the totem pole status, I settled down to work. My biggest problem is money. I keep writing checks and forgetting to record them in my checkbook and have to call home for money to cover checks. The last time this happened, my mother refused to help out and told me to get a part-time job."

Since many states do not allow minors to have checking accounts, this new form of money management leads many novices to over-draw their accounts. They soon learn the knack, but hopefully, budgeting money was learned during high school or before.

The adjustment of being on one's own is made easier when high school students take responsibility for their grades, money management, and their health and safety.

"My father decided that since I insisted on being treated as a young adult, I should be accountable for my teeth. He said he would pay for all unavoidable dental expenses—check-ups and extractions. If I got cavities because I ignored dental care, the expense would be mine. Naturally, I thought he was a miser, but since I didn't want to spend my money on dentists, I flossed and brushed without being nagged. I haven't had a cavity for two years. My dad is so pleased with himself because he invented a new way to get me to accept responsibility."

Jody has worked after school in a real estate office for the last two years. "I like having my own money and I haven't missed any social life because of my job. I'm experienced in dealing with all sorts of people. Mostly, I've learned to fend off creeps. You would be surprised how many 'nice' men like to grab young girls. I've developed a 'cigarette as a shield routine,' 'the slipping sideways when a lunge is coming,' and 'the straight-forward (would your boss-wife-kids like to know you're a letch?)' approach. I'm going to be a writer one day and expose these kind of men."

Most of the jobs available to teenagers are not rewarding in the sense of making the worker feel significant. Fast-food chains are a case in point. Employees often feel like extensions of the automatic machines which cook the food. The boredom of doing the same mechanical acts is difficult to adjust to. Parents can be sympathetic but, at the same time, can help the teenager to understand that most jobs have an element of boredom, another reality message that will make the jolt of entering the adult world not quite so surprising.

Ron, sixteen, was highly enthusiastic over his new job as a cook with a fast-food chain. He had been looking for a summer job for a month and was beginning to feel discouraged. He had seen television commercials of this particular chain and all the employees were singing, smiling, and seemed to love their work. Ron loved his job for a total of two days. At first, the mechanized machines seemed like a challenge and the beeps and buzzes were fascinating. The particular restaurant he worked for was the third most successful fast-food restaurant in three states. They were constantly busy. Ron liked the idea of working, but he began to feel like a machine. He said, "We were all bored to the point of tears. There was a digital clock which everyone looked at every two minutes, counting the time until our shift was over. When I got my first paycheck, I didn't feel any excitement. It seemed like I had lost something of me."

The increasing boredom pushed Ron into looking for some other job. He found one at a gas station and loved the work from the beginning. "I get to talk with different people all day. I can joke and laugh with the mechanics. They like their job and teach me things. I can lube cars, change tires, and give directions. Most of all I am with people. I work every day after school and my boss wants me back next summer. I will never, never work for any place that makes me into a machine."

Many adults have had a first job experience in gas stations, and most say it was a wonderful time, mostly because of the constant activity and the opportunity to learn how to deal with people.

Peer Loyalties

Teenagers are mostly self-absorbed because of the variety of feelings that occur simultaneously within their psyches. The banding together with peers, who are themselves struggling with normal growing pains, gives teenagers a sense of belonging. While teenagers may rebel from and deny parents' life-styles, they, at the same time, tend to be total conformists. They strictly follow the unwritten membership guidelines of their peer group. The fear of being outcasts pressures members of high school cliques to assume similar mannerisms of speech, dress, and even coded walking patterns. Some groups will loudly proclaim their disdain for regular teenage dress patterns and invent possibly wild or outlandish styles of their own. However, they do not dare to stand out except within the safety of a group.

The conformity and rigid loyalties of high school cliques satisfy the teenagers' need for bonding while they are relinquishing their bonds with parents. The need to be connected is so intense that some youngsters have transitional bonding with just one friend, a fantasy idol, one record, certain items of clothing, an animal, or even a book that they compulsively reread. This period of outer-directed bonding can be seen as a search for a temporary haven to fortify teenagers before they begin a concentrated effort to form intimate heterosexual connections. Although the intense surrender of the self to peer groups may seem alarming, it is another important developmental passage in becoming a separate person. Peer identity may look and sound superficial and degrading, but it marks an authentic period of growth.

Some teenagers do not become involved with peer groups and seem content to pursue interests on their own, following a different, inner music. They may have quietly debonded from their parents and feel secure enough to depend on their own inner resources before heterosexual involvements begin. This is often the case with gifted children, who frown on their peers' need for continual approval and acceptance from the crowd. Creative children have their own approval systems, since they enjoy the delight of using their talents.

Dealing with Love and Sexuality

Intrinsically involved with the emotional tasks of debonding, finding acceptance with peers, and dealing with schoolwork, love and sexuality are basic concerns of teenagers.

As experienced adults, we know that teenage love is usually not enduring, and is frought with jealousies, misunderstandings, and possessiveness. However, in order to learn mature judgment of others, discover which traits and qualities are preferable in a mate, and learn how to share, compromise, and become loving friends, teenagers must have extensive contact with many people. They must invest strong love feelings in their current choices if they are going to have the motivation to strive for intimacy. They will never learn the responsibility of commitment and the give-and-take balance in relationships if they treat love as a meaningless stage they are passing through.

The force of love is a powerful element since childhood—in everyone's life. Babies take in love, and, as they grow, learn to give it back. Children are deeply loving with their parents. Many grade-school children fall in love with all the gentleness and sweetness of adults. Romantic attachments are possible at any age. The upsurge of sexuality in adolescence, and the feelings that accompany debonding from the family push teenagers to place the original family love onto other people—lovers and friends. The love teenagers invest during these years has been with them since childhood, and their love feelings are absolutely authentic. Understanding parents respect the intensity of teenage love, even if they know it is not permanent. Love feelings are perceived as lasting "forever" to a young person enraptured by another.

"Our shy son didn't date until he was sixteen, and then fell madly in love with his first girlfriend. She lived close by and was often at our home. My husband and I thought she was a shallow, deceitful, and conniving person, obviously using Kirk for her convenience. She ordered him around, borrowed his precious possessions, and kept him in a state of insecurity by teasing him about other boys. He was oblivious to her power over him. I told him she would break his heart and he said, 'I know, but I can't help loving her.'

"My husband and I decided to mind our own business as it seemed ludicrous to try to stop him from seeing his great love. It wasn't easy for us to be pleasant to her when she smiled insincerely at us like we were a couple of old dopes. Of course, she eventually got tired of her slave and dropped him, refusing to return borrowed objects and snubbing him when he telephoned her. He was devastated. We were overjoyed that it was over, but couldn't say, 'We told you so.' Both of us had been in love with heartbreakers when we were young and recovered. He was much more cautious with his next girlfriend, who turned out to be a very kind young lady."

"Our daughter's boyfriend beat her up after an argument over her flirting with another boy," said parents of a seventeen-year-old. "My husband telephoned his parents and they refused to believe their son would hit a girl. We insisted that she break off with him, but they share a locker in school, think they are good friends and, besides, our daughter forgave him. She said he felt terrible about losing his temper and would never hit her again. We read articles on physical abuse which documented that men who hit women continue to use this power in order to control women even when they promise to change their behavior.

"The boy called my husband and made an appointment with him.

We hated him for blacking our daughter's eye and didn't want to ever see him again. My husband felt he should give the boy an opportunity to explain himself since he acted manly by confronting the problem. He apologized profusely, convincing us to allow him to date our daughter again. They still go steady, but I don't trust his lack of control. Our girl confesses that she placates him in order to avoid his jealous and possessive reactions to normal social situations. We don't want her to love this person, but cannot moderate her feelings, nor lock her in her room. We hope that when she goes away to school next year, the romance will dwindle. If she picks another possessive type, I'm going to suggest psychotherapy so she can discover why she chooses such suffocating relationships."

Teenagers take their love interests very seriously. They are extremely sensitive when others tease them, degrade the authenticity of their feelings, and generally scoff at their rapture and pains.

Some parents diminish teenage romance by labeling it "puppy love," desiring to protect their children from the pain of obvious future rejection. This plan does not work because teenagers fall in love anyway. Protecting them from cruel or manipulative people doesn't give them the opportunity to develop skills needed to overcome loss, deal with loneliness, or readjust self-esteem after a rejection.

There is no such thing as unreal love. Love is the core feeling of life and is enriched first by family bonding and later by love relationships outside the family. Parents who love each other can empathize and sympathize with their children's romantic attachments. The feeling of adoration which accompanies love binds people together and motivates them to further understanding and care. Parents will earn respect and future rebonding if they allow teenagers the dignity of love and are kindly sympathetic when inevitable discord and rejection happen, causing true grief over loss.

John and Marcie, both fifteen, felt drawn to each other since they both felt like strangers, newcomers in a large high school. They talked for hours on the telephone, confiding secret feelings. They ate lunch together in the cafeteria and walked with each other to classes. John's father was touched and pleased to see his son so much in love. The father and son talked about the sweet feelings and mysterious closeness which evolves between people in love.

John invited Marcie to the school dance. He bought her a bracelet, took her to dinner before the dance and was generally feeling like he was in heaven. The night after the big event, Marcie called John to tell him she wouldn't be seeing him anymore. No explanation. He was confused, shocked, hurt, and tearful. His father was just as upset as John. After the tears, John felt angry and resolved to never fall in love again.

John's father decided that he had been too hopeful that this relationship would be long-lasting. "I got too enthusiastic. I should have prepared John about the fickle feelings of young people. The next time I'll be pleased for him, but stay more on the sidelines. My own romantic nature clouded my own thinking."

John went through a depression and the normal mourning feelings after the loss of love and dreams. He felt angry at all females and particularly at Marcie for abruptly dropping him. He didn't enjoy the lesson he learned which he described as, "learning to tone down my expectations with a girl." The experience was hurtful but not ultimately harmful. He recovered, receiving sympathy from his father and support from his friends. He decided to try to become pals with some girls in order to understand the way women think. He thought he was too young to try to find "forever" love because it hurt too much to suffer the rejection.

A young teenage boy who makes himself vulnerable by risking the gentle feelings of love needs approval from both parents. If they play down his feelings in an attempt to buffer possible rejection, he will then assume he has few rights to other feminine-labeled feelings as well, such as fear, trepidation, distrust, sadness, or joy. He is once more left with his one culturally approved masculine feeling— aggression. Fortified by the instinctual drives of adolescence, aggression is often turned back on the self, causing outright suicide or "accidental" vehicular death.

The same intensity which teenagers experience with romance is invested in their homofilial friendships. Their loyalty bonds, compassion, and precious trust are shared with friends, excluding parents. A parent's criticism of one's teenage friends is taken as a personal attack on oneself and one's judgment. Teenagers choose friends who they think are similar to them in interests, ideals, and dreams. They must be free to discover that their choices are correct or frustratingly wrong.

Generally, teenagers choose friends who are acceptable to parents. If, however, your children are attracted to people who are definitely into destructive behavior and you know trouble will occur, you have every right to interfere.

"My parents laid down the law about one of my girlfriends. She drove her car like a crazy person and they told me I couldn't ride with her. The way they put it was that they valued my life and I should have enough love for myself not to take ridiculous risks with a person who couldn't handle a car. They made me mad because I really like my friend, but they were right about her driving. I like them because they explain why I can't do something instead of just saying I have to do what they want."

Trials, Dilemmas, and Pressures

In mid-adolescence, many young boys are more than ready for sexual experimentation, whereas usually young girls are far less interested in "going all the way." The pressures for sexual experimentation can lead to confusions, a sense of inferiority if one does not join in "what everyone is doing," and some impulsive decisions similar to the following story.

A young woman recounted that her sixteen-year-old boyfriend had used the line that intercourse would be easy with him because he had a nice, small penis. He was an exciting kisser and adept at the moves of light petting. One evening when her single-parent father was out of town, the fifteen-year-old girl decided to "let it happen." She bullied her younger sister into staying in her room under threat of death and prepared the scene. She had a case of beer ready which she assumed they would drink before "it" happened. She put on her scantiest blouse and shortest shorts, lit some candles, and waited.

When her smooth-talking boyfriend arrived, he appeared somewhat nervous and ill at ease. She rushed around opening beers and then excused herself to douse too much perfume on her shoulders. After several shared beers and languid posing on her part, her "lover" suddenly remembered that he had to get the car home for his parents—a convenient excuse. The girl felt befuddled and rejected after all her elaborate planning and the decision to give up her virginity for love. She couldn't figure out what she had done wrong.

During the next few weeks, her boyfriend continually involved them in group activities as he became more and more distant, finally breaking off their semi-steady arrangement.

Several years later they met at a party, and he confessed that she had scared him with her obvious and aggressive plan for sex. He told her that he had been a virgin himself and hadn't the slightest notion of how to begin or what was expected of him. He apologized for not having been honest at the time, and they both shared a laugh about their mutual incompetence. She thanked him for saving her from getting involved before she was emotionally ready for sex. She told him it wasn't until she was seventeen that she had intercourse, at which time she was able to handle the practical side of birth control, the emotional investment and commitment, as well as the mutual pleasure involved. Such a commitment was far better than "giving in" in order to please an insistent boyfriend.

Many mid-adolescent girls complain about the constant male pressure to have intercourse. They don't feel ready for sexual union but enjoy kissing and being close. They are unaware of the intense penis sensations such love play arouses in boys and cannot understand why boys can't enjoy just necking and leave it at that. Boys feel teased and frustrated and continue the pressure. Since sexual desire and the wish for release are normal, the dilemma is profound for both sexes.

Many young females (fourteen to sixteen years of age) do not feel ready for intercourse and wonder what all the clamor is about. Young boys feel intense sensations in their penises and want nothing more than to get inside a female, creating a dilemma. Young people should have an avenue of sexual expression, simply because sexual desire is a healthy, normal appetite, present from birth. Young people also have an intense need to express their love for each other.

Facing the Issue

Parents cannot hide their heads in the sand and count on luck that their children will abstain from sexual experimentation until they reach maturity and are capable of handling the emotional risks and commitments that are connected with sexuality.

Today's teenagers think it absurd that older generations waited to have sex (or so they say) until marriage. The current generation has been reared in an atmosphere of immediate gratification, fear of impending war, and sexually stimulating musical lyrics, movies, and magazines. Why should they wait? They do not see any reason to put off pleasure, nor do they suffer from unreasonable guilt. As we have discussed before, their sexual urges and needs are not of their doing, but a natural, biological force.

Because parental supervision lessens during high school years, teenagers will find a way to experiment sexually. Setting strict curfews in hopes of heading off sexual activity has been a joke among young people for years. If they are interested enough in sexual experimentation, the time of day or night is insignificant. With millions of homes and apartments left empty every day when parents leave for work, young people can easily find safe and convenient places to explore their sexuality. The popular vans that many teenagers drive have a nickname of "traveling bedrooms."

Since most teenagers will find a way to experiment with sex, at least to some degree, sexual education is an urgent, ongoing necessity. Adolescents must learn to deal with the consequences of their behavior and understand that sexual experimentation has specific responsibilities connected with it. Teenagers want everything to be spontaneous and natural. They think that planning ahead with birth-control devices is too premeditative. They believe that pregnancies magically will not happen to them. Even some girls who have delivered babies refuse birth-control counseling because "It won't happen again."

Parents can help their teenagers prepare for their sexual lives by explaining that no method of birth control is 100 percent effective. Unknown to many people who use the withdrawal method (male removing his penis before ejaculation), some sperm can leak out without the male sensing it, which can cause pregnancy. A trip to Planned Parenthood is invaluable in order to learn the varieties of birth-control methods available. They also have concise information about venereal diseases, their symptoms and treatments.

In talks about life with their children, parents have a unique opportunity to explain what sex should and should not be: that sexual intercourse is not just a release from sexual tension, but an act that involves mutual sharing, respect and consideration, tenderness and passion. Boys should learn from fathers that it is unethical to seduce and use women solely for their own pleasure. Parents should explain that sex should never be used to placate a partner, keep a partner's affections, or gain popularity; such use makes sexual activity a barter. No one should have intercourse unless he or she is prepared with birth-control devices, a fact which should be repeated often to sexually active young people (they have as many misconceptions about birth control as little children do about birth). No one should demand sex, using it as a weapon or threat against loss of love. No one should have sex with only selfish motivations, using a partner as a masturbatory tool. No one should join in sexual activities because of peer pressure to belong.

Sex should be a mutual exchange of tender, caring passion whereby two people express their love through physical caresses. Sex should be joyful, mutually pleasurable, involving concern for a partner's pleasures. Sex should be considered a treasured gift between two people and should be connected with good, loving feelings.

Your views on sexual expression and birth control can be discussed with teenagers when they know you will respect their opinions. Conversations about the morality of sexual sharing can be included in talks about planning for the future, treating sex as another facet of becoming an adult.

"We have our own ethical system in my high school crowd," said Peter. "No one admires anyone for sleeping around. We think sex is okay when couples love and respect each other."

During a parent-teenage seminar on solutions to generational differences about sexual morality, a seventeen-year-old girl related, "My parents decided that my boyfriend and I were making love. I don't know how they knew, but they were right. My mother said she understood our wish to enjoy sex, but that we had to be responsible. We'd been counting on luck when it came to birth control. My dad said we had to consider our futures—too young to be parents, no money for abortions, and he wasn't going to be responsible for anyone's baby. I'm on the pill now and take it with my vitamins.

"My parents may be considered too liberal by some because they let it be known that my room was private. They don't want us parking in some secluded spot and getting mugged. Their unspoken invitation to enjoy lovemaking in the safety of their house has made my boyfriend and me respect ourselves and them in a special way. They removed the forbidden quality from sex and since then, we don't seem so frantic about it."

In response, a father said he could not condone his unmarried children having sex in his home. "If teenagers are going to express their sexual longings, they should make adult arrangements. A couple should pool their money and rent a motel room, safe from harm. I'm against high school kids having intercourse, but I know there is no way to stop them. I'd rather they pay their own way and at least be safe and comfortable."

Another student recounted that she had tried intercourse a few times because she really wanted to please her boyfriend. "I really didn't enjoy it and finally told him we would have to wait until I felt more interested. I thought if he really respected me he wouldn't pressure me to have sex if it only gratified him. He agreed, although reluctantly. I feel lucky that I didn't get pregnant the few times we took a chance."

An adult asked why they took such a risk without using any birth control devices.

"We just didn't plan to go so far and the reality of a possible pregnancy seemed far away at the time," was the girl's reply.

A woman in her forties addressed the group saying, "When I was a teenager, most of my friends refrained from intercourse because of the fear of pregnancy and the options. In those days people either married hastily or disappeared to a home for unwed mothers. I married much too young because I couldn't wait to have sex. I thought I was in love, but it was actually sexual frustration. Today, the notion of getting married to have legal sex seems absurd. My children look for respect, friendship, loyalty, mutual interests, and good sex with their partners. They don't put sex in a forbidden compartment any more, and I think their attitude is healthier than my generation's. The main problem I see is their unconcerned attitude about birth control. We have the responsibility to teach prevention of pregnancy instead of looking for methods to stop sexual experimentation."

If you wish your children to abstain from intercourse, you should be prepared to explain why. "Just because it's right" does not hold enough conviction for today's knowledgeable teenagers. They will want to know what they should do with the insistent urges in their bodies.

"I asked (you don't tell anymore) my teenagers to wait until they felt secure with their identity before they had intercourse," one mother said. "Making a decision about sexuality seems easier to me if young people choose to experiment from a position of strength, instead of having intercourse to prove they are mature. I think when people give themselves sexually, they feel vulnerable and uniquely bonded. Sexual enjoyments should be practiced with some relationship security—that it will have some future. Younger people are trying out romantic attachments, and learning to be intimate can be short-circuited if they use sex to become closer.

"My opinion is that they should learn to be loyal friends first, let love grow on that foundation and, when they have learned to know and trust each other, sexual expression can be a part of their deepening relationship. My children see that my husband and I really love each other on many levels, as partners *and* lovers. I want them to have respect for growing a deeply involved love and friendship relationship which includes sex after some depth has been achieved. I think our society emphasizes intercourse as a panacea for good relationships instead of holding up friendship love as a value. I think my reasoning is sound and my children listened intently. I can only hope they will consider my opinion when they choose their personal sexual behavior."

Whereas parents fear pregnancies, young people do not consider the consequences of unprepared-for-intercourse. What compromise can be made between unpremeditated intercourse and possible repression brought about by total sexual abstinence? One solution is to educate youth about their responsibilities with regard to birth control. Another is to explain that sexual expression does not have to be penis-vagina directed. To have this narrow orientation defines sex as a predominately genital activity, rather than including the whole body. Mutual masturbation does not lead to pregnancy, but it does teach couples to be sensitive and thoughtful about each others' feelings and sensations. Both sexes learn about the sensual pleasures that can be enjoyed by their entire bodies when they give each other massages. Dancing can also be encouraged as a form of sexual release through sublimation—it's fun and good exercise as well.

Young people are often drawn into intercourse as an easy method of feeling close and accepted. It is simpler to learn physical intimacy than to work on emotional intimacy. Teenagers are used to quick solutions, but working on the art of emotional intimacy (exposing one's secret self and longings) requires time and patience. Young people love often and intensely, but do not become informed about each other, knowing that they don't expect to make lifelong commitments at this age.

We cannot protect our children from the hurts and rejections in their love lives. If they experiment with sex, the least we can do is state our preferences, educate them about practical and emotional responsibilities, and trust them to make sound decisions. As a rule, they do not want to tell parents about their sexual activities, nor can parents intrusively demand information.

The attitude of the new generation is not "One mistake will stay with you forever," as in past generations. If they contract venereal disease or become pregnant, they should be able to come to parents for advice and emotional support. As a part of dealing with reality, children should participate in the financial expenses incurred by irresponsible behavior. There is nothing as good as working to pay for their own bills to teach young people cause and effect.

Intellectual Growth

As puberty begins, growth occurs in the teenagers' ability to notice connections and think things through; they acquire perceptive intellectual abilities. This awakening of thought processes escalates during mid-adolescence.

Teenagers, depending upon variances in growth, genetic givens, and environmental stimulation, begin a secondary thought pattern. A child thinks, "I want." A teenager thinks, "How can I perform successfully to get what I want?" Secondary thinking involves the ability to imagine concepts and abstractions, pose hypothetical questions and answers, make logical deductions from scattered information, figure out solutions, imagine creative ideas, and think ahead to the future regarding consequences of behavior. These abilities direct teenagers' interest to new ideals and ideologies.

Their questing minds challenge the present system and get stimulated into grandiose visions of improving the world. They daydream schemes which will gain them personal fame and fortune, or imagine sacrificial acts to benefit humankind. Goals seem limitless. They begin to wonder and worry about the meaning of life itself, and theirs in particular. *Who* am I? *Why* am I? *What* am I doing here? Such are the ponderings of youthful minds as they approach problems with a novel and exciting freshness.

Before they can possibly find constructive solutions to current dilemmas, they must criticize and dissect the status quo. This upsurge in intellectual abilities parallels physical and sexual growth. All three of these components of human development give impetus to the teenagers' task of debonding from parents and leaving childhood behind.

A teenager's new ability to think more maturely can be an exhilarating time for parents and an opportunity to validate a young person's mind as he or she gallantly tries out new ideas. The teenager really does not seek to destroy parental ideals but wants room and acceptance to air opinions—another form of delineating himself or herself as a separate individual. When parents respect the next generation's ruminations and their formulations of ideas for adulthood, they take the opportunity to lay the groundwork for future rebonding.

This is the time when parents can encourage teenagers' creative ideas, whether in music or art, in inventions, or in pursuing other endeavors. Using one's intellectual capacities, learning to devise new formulas, discarding unworkable ideas, and producing unique products give young people an injection of healthy, earned self-esteem. Parental praise and encouragement only enhance the teenagers' abilities to inquire into, investigate, expand on, and come up with new ideas. A bonus of increased intellectual activity is the teenagers' heightened sense of humor, which he can now share on an adult level.

The process of intellectual thought opens up a new arena for family interaction which, because it has no qualities associated with childhood, is safe territory for teenagers. The ability of parents and children to talk on an equal basis, without the emotional attachments of childhood, marks the opening of new horizons for family members. This type of relating lacks the sometimes sticky sensual attachments that exist in early childhood between parents and their opposite-sex children.

Physical Well-Being

Teenagers' physical health is important to their well-being. Annual physical and dental checkups are necessary for peace of mind and preventive health care. Because of mistrust of authority figures, many teenagers shun medical and dental checkups, often fearing that the doctors will discover some dread disease which teenagers would rather remain ignorant about. Some teenagers may feel uncomfortable with the physician who has been treating them since infancy and should be allowed to change doctors if they wish.

An understanding pediatrician we know who specializes in adolescent medicine routinely tells his patients that they do not have cancer, diabetes, venereal disease, tapeworms, brain tumors, or unusual genital development. He says that although most teenagers maintain a stance of cool indifference to this news, he can feel them giving a big inward sigh of relief. Discuss this comforting tactic with your family doctor and ask him or her to give periodic reassurance to your teenager, who will believe a doctor's word about the absence of fatal disorders more readily than your own.

If a teenager has a weight problem, a physician who understands the peculiarities of adolescents will be most beneficial. Learning about dieting from a professional carries more conviction than hearing about calories from parents. Fat teenagers are unhappy even if they hide their sadness from the family. Concerned parents compound the pain by constant nagging, and parents who try to ignore the issue by continually buying tempting high-calorie foods are of no help either.

A disorder that mainly affects mid-adolescent girls is anorexia nervosa. It is a form of self-induced starvation which, if untreated, can and does become fatal. The affected girl has a delusional view of her body, seeing it as grossly overweight. She starves herself into a skeletonlike, ghostly figure. Food becomes disgusting, but the anorexic victim will occasionally gorge herself, then feel guilty for having given in to her base appetites, throw up the food, and become even more stringent about her starvation diet.

This disease requires immediate psychiatric care. The underlying motivation for such self-induced starvation is usually a deep unconscious fear of growing into womanhood. The fear is so buried that only a professional can uncover it and lead the girl back to normalcy, which sometimes takes a long time. However, the expense incurred in treatment is necessary because the disorder is deadly.

Teenagers' physical health requires as much attention as their emotional and intellectual growth. They often do not eat the right foods, get enough exercise, or pay attention to proper hygiene. Parental nagging is perceived as "be like me" which contradicts the young person's need to be different. The objective physician can be drafted to remind teenagers of their need to practice good health habits, which effectively removes parents from the position of controller.

FIVE

How to Talk with Teenagers

This subject doesn't have to be solemn and fraught with complexities. Teenagers who feel respected enjoy talking with adults and are eager to try out their increased verbal skills, which grow along with their maturing intellectual capacities.

The Listening Child

Parents, by necessity, do a great deal of lecturing to young children in order to teach them family rules, cooperation with others, and manners to use as their world expands to involve peer play, school, and social activities.

During the family bonding years parents answer innumerable questions posed by the curious young. They are accustomed to fascinated attention by their youngsters as the children impatiently gather information, always ready with further requests for details. Preschool children depend on and unconditionally believe all adult explanations. They are usually quite surprised when they enter school and discover that strange adults and new playmates have information which does not match up with what they have been told at home.

All cultures have set explanations for certain universal events, stories about the tooth fairy, the Easter bunny, and Santa Claus; the pledge of allegiance and the national anthem; and holiday traditions of great variety give structure to a world that poses many questions. Children, in their attempts to adjust to new situations and groups, cling to these familiar traditional beliefs for security. Any differences in opinion and tradition between families are ignored in the service of quasi-bonding with classmates.

Elementary school children spend six or seven years listening to teachers giving instructions without much opportunity to express opinions. The noise explosion at recess reveals their need to talk, scream, and yell. Children passively receive information while watching television and quickly learn that viewers do not talk back to the set.

During early adolescence, when intellectual abilities begin to mature, junior-high pupils are granted freedom to question and comment in the classroom. Girls, usually ahead of boys, may begin to sort out and judge parental viewpoints.

Once the years of high school begin, the mid-adolescent's time to speak out has arrived. High school students, who have been obediently listening, following directions, and accepting verbatim adult commands for fifteen years, abruptly discover their new talent of reasoning out, doubting, and challenging old ideas. They feel, and rightly so, that it's their turn to talk, and they want an agreeable audience. After all, they have been attentive and accepting of adults' pronouncements for many years. It's reasonable to assume that they would desire the same in return.

Most teenagers in the process of debonding are unafraid to express views opposed to those of their parents, because the fear of rejection is not as strong as before. As they distance themselves, it is natural for them to criticize parents in order to claim their right to be different. The debonding years are a time when communication between parent and child takes on a more equal status, with the teenager trying to take over the podium—though insecure, half-informed, idealistic, strident, unsure, and always fluctuating.

The Listening Parent

As we said before, parents' roles constantly change as children move ahead in their development. The role parents must play for teenagers changes from that of dispenser of directions to listener to new ideas, opinions, and criticisms. This new position is difficult for many adults to assume because it is so dissimiliar to the secure position of the always-knowing parents of the childhood years. Parents who make the adjustment and encourage differences of opinion gain respect and set the stage for the rebonding which occurs once their offspring reach adulthood. Parents who cannot accept their teenagers' independent viewpoints often erect barriers of silence which are never scaled, thus missing out on future reconciliation between generations.

Just as teenagers cannot control their physical and sexual maturation, they likewise have no control of the natural increase in their intellectual reasoning. They must use their new skills in an atmosphere of acceptance in order to become functioning adults. They are the authority figures and parents of the future, apprenticing in all facets of maturity.

Learning to Listen

The art of listening can be learned. It requires putting aside the wish to be the admired center of attention, impatience connected with the desire to interrupt, and respect for the speaker. Listening means being alert to the speaker's words and expressions, not glancing around, yawning, or spacing out. Listening to teenagers requires adults to give up defensive bristling if an opinion is in direct opposition to their beliefs. An opinion need not be threatening, since it is only a verbal expression of an idea. Genuine listening means objectively weighing the speaker's thoughts instead of arbitrarily dismissing the validity of opinions even before they have been fully stated.

Listening with an open mind is easy when parents understand that teenagers are trying on new ideas, rather than rigidly maintaining a set view of life. They may defend an idea with great vehemence and conviction one day and discard it the next. In order to test a new point of view, they must believe in it completely. They have the right to discard ideas without being teased or made to feel they have lost face.

Just when young peoples' minds are awakening to the infinite possibilities of life, the parents' system of values and ethics is most likely solidified. Criticism of parental systems can be easily withstood if those systems are sound and workable. If the system is faulty, perhaps a teenager can offer constructive suggestions. Adults aren't perfect, and teenagers enjoy testing reactions when they point out discrepancies. Adults can accept criticism with good humor if they are comfortable with their imperfections. However, if adults try to maintain the illusion of being perfectly mature and error-free, criticism will be perceived as an artillery attack.

One evening, a father noticed his son peering intently at him while they were discussing the ecological damage done over the past generations. The father was in agreement with his son's disgust over the greed of big business. The boy seemed slightly surprised that his father readily agreed with him. He wanted some area of dispute in order to feel separate. He finally said, "You know, you have the weirdest veins in your legs." What is a parent to do? This father was well aware of the boy's need to devalue him. He calmly replied, "Oh, that's because I'm a decrepit old guy, or it could be a sign of creeping insanity." They both laughed and moved on to talk about issues of more meaning and interest to the curious teenager.

Wise parents do not allow themselves to get sidetracked by becoming defensive when teenagers criticize their appearance. A sense of humor is the most valuable tool when dealing with personal criticisms. The teenager is really testing to see if he or she can comment negatively and still be accepted. Because parents have been saying for fifteen or sixteen years, "Stand up straight! You'll freeze that way! Your face is dirty! Wash your hands! Comb your hair! You look awful! Listen to me!" adolescents want to have their chance to comment on parental quirks and faults. Parents still love their children while pointing out their flaws, and children still love their parents when they return the favor. Fault-finding is simply not a big deal unless parents make it so. Teenagers have enough feelings to deal with without being forced to feel guilty about their need to dethrone parents.

A mother recounted that her twin boys had always loved her meals. Suddenly, at fifteen, they began to complain and criticize her every effort. Instead of being resentful over this new situation, she cheerfully removed herself from the kitchen and suggested that the boys learn to cook. Her husband joined his sons and taught them some basic dishes. The boys learned necessary skills, enjoyed the camaraderie with their father, and, most importantly, felt grown up. Mothers' bestowal of love is equated with serving food. This woman recognized that her boys wanted to be independent from her and this need expressed itself in regard to her role in the kitchen. She was listening to their debonding needs in her own way, responded with a creative idea, and avoided feeling attacked.

Teenagers appreciate parents who listen to their opinions and then elicit further conversation by asking questions. This way they feel as though they are being treated with some importance, rather than being downgraded to the status of a child as parents tell them something in an authoritative manner. Questioning rather than lecturing softens the image of the "always-right" adult.

"I'm buying a motorcycle on time," boasts a daughter to her mother, proud of her first summer job.

To respond with, "You can't afford it" puts down the girl's decision, making her feel stupid.

"Have you budgeted that expense?" or "Have you figured out how long it will take you?" stimulates a person either to show how responsible she is or to look again at what may be an impulsive decision.

Such questioning builds trust in teenagers. They want the security of knowing that parents won't jump all over them when they make pronouncements. Being able to rely on nondefensive reactions from parents makes adolescents feel respected.

Small children are interested in all the stories that parents tell them. Teenagers are not interested, and are turned off by adult reminiscences about their own teenage years, unless such memories are used to reveal that all adults once suffered adolescent confusions. Interest in the parent as a person with an interesting past is rekindled in later years. "When I was your age, I did this and that" is boring to teenagers, because it carries the unspoken message that the parent handled life more successfully than the teenager and is therefore superior. Teenagers, distancing themselves from their "old" parents, are uninterested in what seems to them the ancient past. It carries no relevance for them.

Equal Status in Conversations

Disagreements about opposing ideas can be discussed with enthusiasm if teenagers feel that their words have as much value as those of adults. Parents who desire to keep a free-flowing, open dialogue between themselves and their young desist from tactics such as, "You're too young to know all the facts," or "That's dumb," or "How delightful to hear the solutions to the world's problems from such an experienced person." How is the young person going to become experienced at delivering opinions if he or she cannot be free to try out ideas with parents?

A couple who had raised four children said they had used an interesting approach during their children's volatile years of debate: they tried to relate and listen to teenagers as if they were guests in their home and someone's else's offspring. "This canceled our taking their criticisms as personal put-downs and gave us room to listen with reason rather than defensively standing up for our principles as if they were invincible. Neither of us minded being wrong, which many parents can't stand, as though it were degrading to admit mistakes."

One father invented a ritual which pleased his teenagers enormously. Depending upon their emotional readiness, he invited his teenagers to openly criticize his parenting. He had divorced their mother when they were small children and, having shared custody rights, had his children with him half of the time. He had remarried, and he and his second wife had another child. He was quite aware of making mistakes in parenting and was willing to let his children express their feelings about him.

They responded suspiciously at first, wanting reassurance that his feelings wouldn't be hurt or that he wouldn't get angry. After he promised that he would listen objectively, the children had the marvelous chance to complain and criticize with total freedom. His oldest daughter had a great deal of long-repressed anger about his divorce and thought that the failure of his first marriage was all her father's fault, a conclusion supported by her mother's inability to accept any blame. It took his daughter about three weeks of evening discussions to recount her grievances from childhood. The second child spent a scant ten minutes grousing about his father's strictness when he was a little boy and then could think of nothing more to say. The third teenager worked through some feelings of jealousy about being a stepchild and his envy toward his half-sister, who got to spend all her time with "his" dad. Since the boy ran out of complaints, he wanted to know if he could bring up more points in the future.

This father, by inviting his children to evaluate him, gave them respectful attention and made them feel special. He acknowledged their right to have legitimate peeves. He felt that the complaining sessions cleared the air and also gave him the chance to correct some misunderstandings about his divorce and remarriage. He apologized when children brought up acts of his that had hurt their feelings. Most children never hear their parents apologize for anything. This family's sense of worth increased by hearing the father's genuine apologies.

This unique approach to respecting young people's feelings, without inflicting defensive posturing, is to be highly recommended. We have used the same ritual with our children. It is amazing to discover what memories teenagers dredge up, and it is also enlightening to hear about one's own irritating mannerisms, keenly observed over the years by alert children. Occasionally they even throw in a compliment!

Teenagers esteem parents who ask their opinions about current events, movies, books, or present-day fads. They are pleased to think that parents are interested in their perceptions and impressions of the world. They feel important when we reveal regard for their viewpoints, without necessarily having to give our opinions, unless asked. They feel they are being talked *with* rather than spoken *to*—a big distinction to young people.

If parents throw off defensiveness, accept criticism with good humor, encourage debate, and remain open to new ideas, teenagers will also include us in conversations about their hopes and dreams for the future. Being included in such talks gives parents the opening to explain the realities of work and the emotional investment required in forming intimate relationships, and also to discuss their values in life.

An atmosphere of noncritical conversation sets the stage for the questions that confront all teenagers: Why are so many adults superserious and solemn all the time? Why are some people so mean and hateful? Does growing up mean losing spontaneity? Why do so many marriages end in divorce? Can love endure? Why is there so much hypocrisy in the world? Why can't people get it together and work for peace instead of stockpiling weapons which can destroy us all? How can they trust again after a friend cheated them or stole a precious possession? What is reincarnation?

Curious teenagers are eager to question and discuss endless topics once they sense parental interest and flexibility. If they feel trusting, they can admit the disappointments and failures that they experience daily. In contrast, children who feel that parents are not on their side because they disallow debate use sarcasm as a weapon, nag, brand or ignore their opinions, will be suspicious about admitting experiences that leave them vulnerable and confused.

Saying "No" without Fear

Every family evolves its own set of rules for behavior, respect, and functioning. Rules give order and security in any social system. Family standards lend dignity to life and provide a structure for members to depend upon.

Children who were reared in the permissive era of past generations floundered with too much freedom. Misguided parents thought that enforcing rules and external controls would damage psychological growth and retard creativity. They produced a crop of spoiled, rude, uncontrolled, and quite unhappy brats. Many of these children of the permissive experiment complained loudly that they felt that parents didn't care about them since they never bothered to give them any guidelines.

Common-Sense Restraints

Today's parents should understand the freedom needs of young people, but also know that they require appropriate restraints. Self-assured parents use their common sense and are unafraid to say "no" when appropriate. Teenagers will resent their parents for turning them down, but that's okay—the anger won't last long. Family love does not exist in a fairytale cocoon, wherein everything is smooth and in total harmony. Being resentful and hostile are emotions that parents and teenagers often feel for each other. The toddler feels frustrated and angry with his restrictive parents too, not knowing that many insistent "no's" save him from physical harm. Parents lived through that anger and should learn to accept the transitory adolescent grudges in much the same casual manner.

Judy, a mother of three, recounts, "It's easy for me to say no when my teenagers ask us to pay for outrageously expensive clothes or inflated concert tickets. We can't afford luxury items like these, even though both my husband and I have good paying jobs. The children know if they want extras, they have to earn the money themselves. Of course, this doesn't stop them from asking. I turn them down matter of factly because financial realities dictate the limits of family spending.

"My predicament occurs when the children pressure me for permission to wear my clothes, use my car or to engage in undefined activities," she said. "Last summer, my sixteen-year-old, Greg, and three other kids, wanted to travel from Chicago to Mexico. They had no knowledge of Mexican highways, insurance, cultural mores, or health precautions. They were just going 'to drive around and have fun.' His arguments were that the other parents gave permission, everyone was healthy and would not succumb to disease, and he deserved to broaden his experiences with travel. My immediate common sense response was that the trip involved too many unknowns for a bunch of immature teenagers. My guilt system said, 'Let him have fun. He's only going to be young once and besides, he'll be mad at you if you stop his adventure.' Greg intuitively knows when I am vacillating and added pressures, reproaching me for my conservative nature, and scoffing at my concerns. My husband interrupted our bickering and said, 'You can't go. You don't have enough information for safe travel in Mexico. Make better preparations for a trip next year and then we'll give permission.' Greg slammed out of the house, sulked around a few days and then forgot about it. I found out later that none of the parents allowed the trip.

"I need more self-assurance when I am faced with decisions in the 'gray' areas," she admitted.

Further discussion revealed that Judy feels intense discomfort whenever her children are angry with her. She goes to any lengths to avoid disharmony, often giving in to their demands, avoiding the natural hostility which occurs when people are frustrated. The children feel smug about getting their own way, but don't respect their mother. They cleverly arrange their demands to coincide with their father's absence since he has no trouble setting standards.

Everyone is angry when their wishes are denied. Learning how to deal with anger and disappointments is a part of growing into a reasonable adult. Judy's fear of anger and the resulting loss of love, discourages her children from developing skills to handle frustration.

"My dad has always been a soft touch," says Karen, "and I could wheedle money and privileges from him by turning on my sweet-little girl voice. He melted and my mother would get furious when he handed me money. I thought my charms were overwhelming. When I started dating I acted the same way with guys in order to get my own way. All I did was turn them off. One boy said I acted like a Southern Belle from the late night movies and I should grow up. I was unprepared to be honest with boys since my dad let me manipulate him for favors. He should have been more firm. The fun I had lording it over my mother seems childish now. It would have been better if I had learned to state my wishes, argue my point and be told no more often."

Most teenagers want parents' trust. They believe that they are capable of making sound decisions and behaving appropriately in all situations. This omnipotent attitude fuels their demands for freedom. Trust is earned by successfully handling graduated freedoms: If a young person promises to call home if he or she is going to be late and does so, trust grows. If the promise is broken, teenagers must learn that their inconsideration only subtracts from parental trust.

Trusting a teenager with a car is an opportunity for the young driver to earn trust by exhibiting careful driving habits, showing consideration by refueling an empty gas tank, and returning the vehicle in a clean condition. Respect for others' property is gained by learning to care for parents' belongings correctly.

"We usually talk over problems in our family, but were having a hard time getting our son to explain his feelings. He acted like he had an automatic right to drive the family car and couldn't understand why we insisted he earn the right by helping with chores. He felt picked on and we felt he was being uncooperative and sullen. I suggested that he wasn't viewing himself as a member of a group of people working together to keep the house in order. He countered that this approach was new for him. I realized that circumstances had given him a distorted view of household responsibilities. Until a year ago we had a cleaning lady who did all the heavy work. We cannot afford this expense anymore and I had assumed our son would smoothly adjust and help out with housework. We straightened everything out by explaining we were not picking on him by requesting his participation in housework, but that we all had to work together to keep the place clean. He grew up in a time of affluence for us and is learning to adjust to living with inflation. Our explanation of changing times, and needing his cooperation, changed his attitude."

In our family, all the children have participated in dangerous sports, including skiing, dirt bike racing, mountain climbing, and backpacking in the wilderness. Thorough instructions, safe equipment, plus good common sense have prevented accidents (so far). However, when two of our teenagers announced they were buying, with their own earned wages, body kites, both of said, "Absolutely not!" Yells of protest about their history of sports safety and about the right to spend their own money as they wished, as well as angry declarations that "Everyone's into body kites" could not persuade us to change our minds. Too many fatalities had occurred in our mountainous area for us to have given our consent. Of course, they were furious and pronounced us old-fashioned and applied other choice epithets in the privacy of their room. They hated us, for a while, but also respected our final decision on the matter. We had total confidence that we were right. Standing firm has nothing to do with winning battles, but rather with being assured enough to say "no" when "no" is appropriate.

Finding the Right Balance

Sometimes parents can be too restrictive because of their own fears and worries about protecting children from emotional harm. If sons and daughters date others who we know will hurt them, saying "no" is inappropriate. They must learn about people on their own. Trying to separate ill-fated couples almost always forces them together, the restrictions adding dramatic romance to a relationship that would die on the vine if parents left teenagers alone to discover their own mismatchings.

Friends become alarmed when they witness a pal involved in a seriously dangerous relationship. They pressure the naive person into examining the consequences of dating someone involved with drugs or criminal behavior.

"My best friend was going with a real scum," reports Ellen, "and she wouldn't believe he was a drug dealer. I confronted her and told her she was getting a bad reputation. I said my parents wouldn't let me associate with her anymore. I was lying but I figured since she liked my folks, this edict would have some clout. She finally came to her senses when her boyfriend was arrested for dealing drugs to junior-high kids. Our group rallied around her but really gave her a hard time about being so stupid."

Sometimes, when a child seems to be heading for serious trouble because of romantic attachments, parents must interfere for their offspring's safety.

"Our son was dating a completely unsupervised girl whose parents didn't care what she did. She drank excessively, boasted about drug experimentation and was known for inciting other kids to vandalism. Our son couldn't explain his attraction to this wild person and he seemed unconcerned about possible troubles, like getting arrested. We took away his car privileges just to see how long they would last without transportation. She 'borrowed' other cars and started picking him up around the corner from our house. It was like living inside a soap opera. Our otherwise intelligent child seemed hypnotized by this delinquent mini-woman. We were sure he would come to bodily harm. Since he appeared to have lost his mind, we took him to a psychiatrist who specialized in adolescent therapy. Our son had weekly sessions for four months, after which he gave up his obsession with the girl and resumed being a normal teenager.

"We were fortunate to find a therapist who explained his methods to us. He said when treating teenagers, the therapy had to be confidential between the patient and doctor. He could not keep us informed nor explain why our son was acting in such a bizarre fashion. Our boy never confided why he became involved or what happened in therapy to change his mind about the girl. We are just grateful that our insurance covered the expense and that it was successful."

If teenagers feel you are really too restrictive, say "no" too often, and don't understand their freedom needs, try to listen to their side about why they should be allowed specific freedoms. Listen with empathy, for they may have some valid points. If parents compromise on some issues, teenagers learn that a logical presentation may gain them some freedom. Compromise from adults does not have to involve a sense of losing, as it exemplifies the willingness to be flexible in the face of sound arguments.

Some teenagers often show a preference for one parent with whom they feel more comfortable discussing problems and decisions. The chosen parent is usually the one who is most in touch with his or her own feelings as a teenager. To be treated as a teenager's confidant, the respector of the young person's secret thoughts and longings, is a special privilege. The other parent need not feel jealous, but might explore the reasons why the teenager does not confide in him or her. The answer usually rests in not listening enough, still giving unasked for advice, the inability to grant trust when it has been earned, and, perhaps, treating teenagers as parental possessions rather than as separate people.

Since talking together is a safe, nonchildish avenue of expression for teenagers, adults must take every opportunity to keep the doors of conversation open. Many times patience will turn to exasperation, but the rewards of inviting exchanges between the generations keep adults young in spirit and alert to changing social values.

Clever teens can trip up parents who give vague rules. "Be nice to your little brother" can be stretched to mean many things, but if you specifically state, "You don't have to like your little brother but you cannot hit him," your rule of nonviolence is clear. If necessary, write down the rules of acceptable behavior, so that teenagers know where they stand.

We emphasize free-flowing communication with teenagers but urge parents not to confuse open talk with license to be rude. Good manners make life pleasant, and all members of a family should learn to be reasonably polite. Children who speak rudely to their parents do not really enjoy this freedom. Interrupting parents at will does not teach teenagers the patience they will need to wait their turn in conversations. Swearing at family members demeans everyone.

Teenagers learn manners by repetition. If they are told often enough to introduce their friends, introductions will become automatic. If "please" and "thank you" are desired amenities in your home, teenagers should be expected to use them routinely, too.

Reciprocal Rights

Parents can live in harmony with teenagers. Understanding the transformation from dependent child to independent adult does not mean parents must live for teenagers.

Reciprocal behavior is one of the elements of a mature adult—the ability to recognize that others require thoughtfulness, consideration, empathy, and privacy. The change from self-centered child to mature youth adult requires years of teaching on the parents' part. While teenagers are experiencing their physical and psychological growth, they absorb the atmosphere of the adults with whom they live. Parents reveal the benefits of reciprocal treatment in relationships by their everyday treatment of their mates, friends, and children. Respect for privacy begets mutual appreciation for privacy. Courtesy engenders thoughtfulness. Empathy stimulates concern. These lessons of mutual respect are often unspoken and may not become apparent in teenagers' behavior until they are young adults.

SIX

Problems, Large and Small

Do you recall the edginess that would swiftly overwhelm you when you were a teenager? This antsy anxiety attacks all adolescents at some time, disrupting their fragile self-control system.

The Itch

Sitting in a classroom on a beautiful spring afternoon stimulates an itch for adventure as well as, sometimes, romance. A balmy autumm evening with nothing to do activates mischievous thoughts. An increase in intellectual capacity and the growth of a sense of humor start teenagers thinking up hilarious (to them) stunts to release pent-up energies.

Creative Mischief

In the old days when our society was mostly rural, teenage mischief was labeled "farm-boy pranks." Feisty boys would work for hours under the cloak of darkness moving a neighbor's outhouse into his front yard, giggling as they imagined the family's consternation the next morning. The label for such pranks graduated to "hooliganism" after families moved to the cities. Exuberant groups of teenagers

101

would delight in dumping garbage on a grumpy neighbor's lawn or in howling through windows in the middle of the night. Most adults will admit to having participated in some teenage acts of gleeful defiance against the adult world with all its stodginess. Misbehavior of this sort is to be expected during the mid-adolescent years.

A woman remembered how in her teenage days she and friends would drive by a group of people waiting at a bus stop. "One of us would shout, with great seriousness, 'Don't you people know this is not a bus stop anymore? It was changed last week!' We would roar away, laughing, as people looked around, confused and half-believing us."

Her husband recalled "mooning" strangers as they stopped at red lights. "Mooning" is exposing buttocks, which can be be quite disconcerting when a person is waiting for a light change, thinking of mundane matters, and is interrupted by the sight of a naked behind.

A pastor in our neighborhood was confounded for months by a group of teenagers. His church has a sign in front of the building with a weekly message lettered for the public, such as, "Pray for them who persecute you" (Matt. 5:44). The next morning the sign would read, "Persecute them who pray for you" (Tmat 4:54). Or "The wages of sin is death" (Rom. 6:23) would be changed to read, "These fogs thawed sin" (Morin 2:63). The pastor was most alarmed when the mischief makers had rearranged the words to connote something sexual. The sign-changing occurred all year and mysteriously stopped when the then current senior class graduated.

Another group delighted in erecting snow sculptures on the high school lawn after a snowstorm. These creations were always sexually explicit, causing the janitor to get busy with his shovel as quickly as possible.

Parents often mutter about why such energies cannot be directed into studies or something constructive, but teenagers believe that their mischief is constructive for them; beside, they love the intrigue of evading capture.

All such mischief is a youthful conspiracy against solemn-faced adults.

Vandalism

Some teenagers express their discontent through threatening acts of aggression far more serious than mischievous pranks.

High school students who are physically acting out destructive wishes will vandalize a building by breaking windows or starting fires. Sometimes they are caught and taken to jail—a consequence they rarely consider.

What should parents do if called by the police about a child's arrest? First, parents must deal with their automatic denial reactions of "My child wouldn't do a thing like that!" Something must have occurred to cause enough suspicion by the authorities to lead to arrest and detainment. Second, parents, in order to deal calmly with the situation, should not take the act as a personal attack on them; it may turn out to be so, but that issue can be confronted later. Third, an arrest for vandalism usually does not mean a permanent black mark on a person's life record, so try to view the incident in the context of the moment. Fourth, if this is a first offense, take your money and bail your child out. Handle the business transaction with the police as quietly as possible, saving comments about the arrest for when you return home. If this problem has become a recurring one, let the delinquent spend the night in an unpleasant cell. Repeated quick rescues teach the child to expect easy forgiveness without any discomfort.

When malicious vandalism happens in neighborhoods, most authorities will settle with the parents out of court, more interested in payment for damages than the wish to penalize young people. All expenses incurred should be paid for by the teenager. Even if parents can easily afford to spend the money, a person does not learn the consequences of his or her behavior if let off the hook with just a verbal reprimand. Parents should insist on repayment, even if the young person must sell a possession or work after school to reimburse them for the amount.

"Our daughter, a girlfriend, and two boys had hung around together since the seventh grade. As teenagers they always had fun going places, looking out for each other, and caused very few problems.

"One night when my husband was driving home on the freeway, he saw a group of kids throwing a dummy off an overpass, causing cars to swerve and almost collide with other vehicles. My husband was certain he recognized our daughter and her friends. When the group gathered at our house later that night he pounced on them. "I saw all of you throwing that thing off the overpass." He was too furious to ask friendly questions like, 'What did you do tonight?' They looked guiltily at each other, giggled, and mumbled about having some fun. "While you were enjoying scaring drivers, consider how you'd feel if one of you were driving, saw a body hurtling toward you, swerved, hit another car, totaled the automobile, and ended up dead," yelled my irate spouse. His vivid description shocked the vandals into realizing their prank was potentially homocidal. We were both disgusted and amazed that this 'nice' bunch of kids could act so cruelly, and told them so.

"After much fidgeting, they promised to act more maturely and asked us not to tell their parents. To pay for his silence, my husband said they would have to make up their harmful actions by doing free work around the neighborhood for a month. He extracted a contract from them to help the neighbors with gardening work, which they did, much to the surprise of the homeowners on our block. We can only assume that they have stopped their malicious pranks and learned to consider their actions.

"Since this incident we have spent considerable time with our daughter and her friends, talking about their options to release excess energies. We do not nag them about their past since they willingly made amends by volunteer labor. They formed a small business which includes snow shoveling, wall painting, and gardening. They make extra money, enjoy working together, and we usually know where they are."

Impulsive vandalism is often committed for thrills, showing off, or the result of too much alcohol intake. Teenagers who destroy property for these reasons can often be redirected into work, forcing them to make financial reparation, reinforcing values about respecting property, and directing their thoughts to how they would feel if victimized by vandals.

There are teenagers who destroy property, set fires, steal expensive objects, or torture helpless people or animals because they are angry at parents or society at large. They require more drastic action than rechanneling energies. There is no stereotyped description available of the teenager who commits crimes because of pent-up rage, but whoever he may be, he needs help.

A mother brought her fifteen-year-old daughter to our clinic because the girl had taken her parents' priceless coin collection and spent the money on treats. The parents suspected that other missing items from their home had been stolen by their daughter. The girl refused to talk to her parents, was furious about being dragged to the clinic, and presented a picture of stoic hostility.

Trained adolescent therapists quickly cut through this kind of chip-on-the shoulder defense. After she was assured of the confidential aspect of therapy, Gail relaxed and admitted taking the coins "on a lark." When asked about angry feelings that could cause such behavior, she poured forth a litany of complaints against her parents. They treated her like a child, restricting her freedom even though she earned privileges by helping with housework and babysitting for her younger siblings. There was no back and forth communication between teenager and parents; only commands and obedience. She got even by stealing their beloved collection.

The therapist requested and received permission to mediate between the client and her parents. They were not cruel adults, but simply had little understanding about a teenager's needs. They were stunned that their daughter held such resentments and seething anger toward them, and agreed to attend a four-hour seminar on how to talk with teenagers. Their knowledge helped them encourage Gail to talk about her feelings, helped them listen with open minds and evolve equitable changes in their treatment of her. Gail stopped stealing as a revenge, and can now express her feelings without fear of censure.

Professional assistance is a necessity if parents cannot initiate talks in order to discover a teenager's source of anger. Once the focal point of rage is pinpointed, verbalized, and solutions are sought, the delinquent acting out usually ceases.

Seeking professional help does not imply parental failure, any more than adults should feel adequate to treat physical injuries. The expense involved is worth it when it stops violent behavior.

Family physicians are often a good referral source for adolescent therapists. Local county medical societies have lists of trained psychiatrists. Friends who have had successful experiences with therapy are an excellent source for therapists. County Social Service Departments give information on health clinics that offer graduated rates according to income.

Small-Time Theft

Petty thievery is a predictable activity of teenagers and reaches its peak between the ages of fifteen and seventeen. Putting something over on the grim grocery store manager is considered great sport.

The phone rang at our house some summers ago.

"Hello, mom," said one of our boys in a tremulous voice. "Ah, we (his brother and himself) just happened to be at the supermarket and wondered if you needed anything."

Since this question was totally out of character and since living through other teenagers' antics had brought a measure of experience, mom said, "Are you calling from the manager's office?"

"Yes."

"Are you supposed to confess to stealing something?"

"Yes."

"Confess."

"We stole two cans of pop, and Mr. White said we had to call home."

"Well, you better apologize and promise not to do it again and tell Mr. White I said to come home."

The manager successfully used this technique with first-time offenders, warning that repeaters would next have to deal with the police. He effectively scared away dozens of first-time shoplifters from further thievery.

The two boys arrived home, white-faced and frightened from the manager's lecture, plus fear of the unknown horrors of parental punishment. They got another lecture from their father, which sank in sufficiently to curb any more attempts to get "free" drinks.

Teenagers are too old to be slapped. Young people respond much better to a few harsh words and explanations about consequences of impulsive behavior than to physical punishment. Grounding them for more than a few days is excessively punitive and causes bitterness instead of comprehension of the faults of their deeds. Stewing over prolonged grounding and suffering feelings of imprisonment make teenagers turn to thoughts of revenge. If parents talk their stupid acts over with them and let them experience some shame about their silly deeds, mischievous adolescents learn to take responsibility for their own behavior.

Shoplifting

Kleptomania, the compulsion to steal, used to be considered a grave psychological problem. In recent years the main motivation is boredom, as young people's leisure time has increased.

A group of six teenage girls had a secret club called "The Double Ks." No one ever knew the meaning of the initials, nor were any new members ever invited to join the exclusive club. The girls lived in a wealthy, big-city suburb, were top students, and were considered popular. They all wore the latest fad fashions, had their hair styled at expensive salons, and drove their own late-model cars.

One day at the local sprawling shopping center, a neighbor spotted one of the girls casually dropping some expensive perfume into her knapsack. The lady then observed how several of the group were distracting salespeople with innocent conversation while others deftly lifted items into purses and under jackets.

The neighbor waited outside the store and confronted the giggling shoplifters. She took them aside and insisted they dump their loot in a shopping bag. She knew the store's policy was "soft" on shoplifters, never prosecuting them for fear of offending the store's wealthy customers. A quick appraisal of the contents of the shopping bag revealed approximately $150 worth of merchandise. The girls stood around, cool and unperturbed by the woman's discovery. She knew all of the girls' parents, and three of the girls had babysat for her. She asked them to meet her at her house, promising them that she really just wanted to talk about the situation, without making judgments.

She returned to the store and approached the manager, telling him that she had just retrieved his goods and asked him to reconsider his store's lax prosecution policy. "If kids know nothing will happen to them, they will feel encouraged to steal," she told the surprised manager.

She had an easy rapport with teenagers, and, after a few minutes of evasion, the girls confided in her. The name of their club was "The Klepper Klub," a play on the word "kleptomania." The goal of the organization was to see how much merchandise two teams of three could grab from a store within thirty minutes. The winning team divided the entire loot, though the items they stole were unimportant to them. Their parents never noticed the excess of expensive goods, as each girl's home was filled with the junk of conspicuous consumption.

They were bored, had no homework after school, didn't have to work because their allowances were more than generous, and confessed to having no challenges in their lives. Shoplifting was a game of chance, a thrill. They all said that they felt as if they really achieved something, had fun, and stole only from large companies. The fact that shoplifters add to everyone's burden since losses are passed along to consumers as higher prices had no impact on children whose parents spent lavishly.

The secretive, forbidden joy of The Kleppers was that they felt important for thirty minutes (every day!) and relieved their tedium. They felt close bonds with each other as they laughed at duped parents, teachers, and neighbors who referred to them as "those bright, sweet, pretty girls." None of them felt mistreated, neglected, or unloved by her parents, nor did any of them particularly fear exposure or punishment.

The neighbor thought awhile, recognizing that there were no levers to use to scare these sophisticated thieves into socially acceptable behavior: the store would not prosecute them, nor would their parents believe the extent of their "good" daughters' criminal jaunts.

Using as a lever their boredom, their need to achieve something different, and the unspoken lack of meaning in their lives, she asked them to try an alternative to their club's activities. "This will be a short experiment in options," she explained. When she first suggested they all visit a nearby nursing home to talk and read to the old people, the girls resisted. Many suburban children rarely see old people and develop a fear of their helpless condition. These girls only occasionally saw grandparents and felt uncomfortable about "touching that old skin." The woman reminded them about their need for challenge and chided them for being afraid of nonthreatening old people.

They visited the nursing home and were all amazed at the deep gratitude the old people showed when the girls merely read them verses in the old greeting cards set up around their night tables. They also discovered that old, wrinkled skin is "soft, like velvet." The lonely occupants of the nursing home, starved for affection, soon pulled out the more generous nature of The Kleppers. The girls formed foster grandchild relationships with many of the patients, and, in doing something of value for others, brought meaning into their own lives. They learned about death, as two of their favorites succumbed before their startled eyes. They learned some history as they listened to stories of pioneer days from people in their nineties. They stopped stealing. No one ever discovered the original goals of The Double Ks, except the neighbor who remained silent.

The girls were leaders in their school, so their encouragement of others to "come and read to the old grannies and grandpas" was quickly picked up as a mutually rewarding volunteer activity. The Kleppers are now career women or married homemakers. They all keep in some contact with their old neighbor who taught them a positive option.

Confronting a Shoplifter

Confrontation is necessary if you suspect that your child and his or her friends are "into" stealing, usually apparent by an excess of expensive objects around the house, or vague explanations of, "Oh, Shelia gave me that the other day." Even though teenagers who shoplift for thrills eventually give up the practice, it is still illegal and unethical to steal from any person or place of business. Stealing is a sign, prevalent in teenagers, of lack of inner controls for socially acceptable behavior. You as parents can help young shoplifters gain self-control, rather than good-humoredly letting them indulge in antisocial acts.

It is advisable to assess your expectations before you confront a teenager about suspected stealing. Confrontation when furious usually leads to yelling, name-calling, severe punishment, and seething hostilities from the accuser and accused.

Confrontations yield better results when approached with calm and confidence. The goal of exposing a person's thievery is to re-educate and reenforce reality. Punishment is appropriate, but rehabilitating the stealer is better achieved in an atmosphere of parental self-control.

A mother related that she had come home early from work and surprised her daughter in the act of removing three sweaters with the price tags still intact. "She quickly left the living room and pretended that nothing had happened. It was obvious she had been shoplifting. If she had made a legitimate purchase, the clothes would have been in a shopping bag and she would have shown me her new acquisitions.

"I was indignant that she was flaunting our years of teachings about honesty and respect. I wanted to slap her around, scream and swear, reduce her to a sobbing apologetic heap, recanting her sneaky ways and force her back to the store in a state of humiliation. That was what I wanted to do. Although I am capable of such strong-armed tactics, I don't like to be out of control and hysterical. I must admit to enjoying the fantasy of pushing her around because it let off my initial rage. I waited a few minutes to simmer down and then felt prepared to deal with her. There was no sense in asking her to prove she had purchased the sweaters. This only encourages lying. Teens, like all children, will lie to avoid punishment, so giving her the opportunity to invent a story seemed a waste of time.

"I knocked on her bedroom door, entered, went to her dresser and pulled out the sweaters. I said, 'You can't keept these because you stole them.' Her reaction was a mixture of exasperation and surprise. Her flimsy defense was that everyone steals and the store could afford to lose a few sweaters. The prevailing code of popularity at her school seemed to be founded on the number of cashmere sweaters owned. This materialistic viewpoint disgusts me and my daughter's acceptance of this kind of superficiality is even more disturbing. I said if she really believed her value rested on her wardrobe, she would have to work to buy such luxuries. She actually believed that shoplifting was not a serious crime.

"I finally impressed her that any theft is serious and that her arguments that everyone steals was untrue and without substance. Without being threatening I announced that she had to live by our rules as long as she lived in our family. She cried when I called the store and told the manager we would be returning stolen merchandise. He was grateful and said he would accept the clothing back without questions. The incident was embarrassing for my daughter but I thought it was a necessary outcome of my confrontation. She seemed relieved that I was firm and confident and unafraid to demand she live within our guidelines. She got a job and somewhere along the line discarded the notion of clothes being equated with self-worth.

"I don't remind her of her foray into thievery or treat her as an untrustworthy person. She earned back my trust and respect by getting a job and responding to my ethics."

We had a sixteen-year-old client who regularly shoplifted after school. She felt no guilt about her thefts. One day she was incensed because her purse was stolen from the school locker room. The therapist said, matter of factly, "Why should you be so upset? After all, it was just a fellow thief, doing what you enjoy." The girl had had the experience of being the victim and was stunned into some empathy for the people she had blithely stolen from. This experience and the unsympathetic attitude on the therapist's part stopped her activities. Even though her motivations and actions were changed because of negative reasons, she did succeed in curbing her criminal behavior. She turned into a very pleasant, honest, hard-working, and successful interior designer—an outcome hard to imagine when she was an unrepentent and uncaring teenager.

Reactions can be handled more rationally if parents remember that a stealing teenager will most likely turn into an honest adult.

Teenagers' sense of right and wrong is shaky. Their childhood conscience grows from external parental teachings of good and bad behavior. These edicts are incorporated into the value system of the child. During the adolescent years, these rules for moral conduct may be temporarily discarded, just as the teenager rejects other parental stances. A peer attitude may be assumed which declares that antisocial behavior is acceptable.

As the young person matures, self-control and discrimination grows and solidifies, forming a personal conscience which dictates correct behavior. As these inner controls strengthen, the dishonest behavior of the past are judged as childish and are replaced with adult codes of socially acceptable behavior.

Reasons for Stealing

If a young person steals to impress or buy friends, new methods of gaining friendships can be discussed. "Bought" friends do not last long, because they soon resent a person who tries to purchase loyalty. Peer friends disappear when a fellow student is arrested and labeled a thief.

A mother of a nineteen-year-old college student related that her son recently confessed that during his sixteenth year he regularly stole tape decks from cars and gave them away to acquaintances on the football team. Recounting his experiences he said, "I felt incompetent because I wasn't a jock and thought generosity would buy acceptance into the athlete's clique. No one asked any questions and they did invite me to party with them. I felt like a big man and was very proud of my adroitness as a car-parts' thief.

"A girlfriend of the quarterback took me aside and really straightened me out. She said I was a fool for stealing, and a total jerk to try to buy friends, and that no one would defend me if I were caught. She told me to make friends by being myself. Her phrase was 'You can't buy a hug, dummo!' She also said that when people accept stolen property they never trust the giver because he might lift something of theirs. She made me ashamed of myself and I quit my career as a thief. I learned to make friends by being a loyal person instead of a weasel. That girl became one of my best friends."

Truancy

Many high school students skip school at some time. Flaunting attendance rules is a way of making a temporary statement that teenagers want to take control of externally imposed rules which they have been obediently following since kindergarten. Always available are several much-in-demand note forgers who excel and delight in duplicating parents' signatures. Such misdemeanors that diverge from socially approved conduct need not cause alarm, since adolescent "kicking up of heels" is universal and soon outgrown.

Teacher-Baiting

Teacher-baiting is another semi-malicious enjoyment of mid-teenagers. This verbal torture game usually takes place when teenagers discover chinks in the knowledge armor of previously "all-knowing" teachers. Boys major in this baiting ritual—and usually with female teachers. Women instructors receive a great deal of unde-served sarcasm, which boys use as a verbal distancing weapon against all mother authority figures during the period of debonding from their mothers. Teachers who understand this maneuver need to develop a smooth banter to stop the baiting, while simultaneously allowing the rebellious student to save face in front of his classmates. If the baiting becomes too hostile or personal, the student usually ends up in the counselor's office, and a parent may be called in to hear complaints about the child's remiss attitude.

Teenagers do not comprehend that grownups can get their feelings hurt, experience humiliation, or feel inferior. Often, explaining the frailties of adults will settle the teacher-baiter down. If he cannot change and continues to practice cruel techniques, he will have to take the consequences—poor grades and sometimes suspension. Gregarious teenagers quickly become bored with freedom from school. They miss the attention of their friends and the bustle of school life. Freedom becomes a jail from which the prisoner urgently desires escape.

"I was suspended for two weeks because I lost my temper and menaced a teacher with my fists," moaned Mike. "I had our apartment to myself, slept in, ate all the time, and watched television for a couple of days. All my buddies were in school so I had no one to play around with. My girlfriend's parents wouldn't allow me to visit her during my banishment from school. I felt lonely, bored, and as if the walls were closing in on me. I wish I had kept my temper or had apologized to the teacher for losing control and stayed in school. All I've learned by my suspension is that I hate being alone."

The Drop-out

Over the last ten years, an increase in the number of high-school drop-outs has caused deep and widespread concern among educators and parents. The decision to leave school, with no plans or hope for success in the job market, seems irreversible and causes much parental worry.

Many drop-outs are not sullen, lazy, or dumb. Many are extremely bright students who cannot stand the boredom of the curriculum, or the coldness and lack of interest displayed by teachers. They feel that "putting in time" is absurd. However, the boredom produced by tedious, meaningless work can cause fatigue, anger, and eventual disillusionment. It may actually be more advantageous for bright, exasperatedly bored students to remove themselves from the dullness of high school and gain some life experiences. The GED (General Educational Development) program is always available to those who leave school and subsequently want a high-school-equivalency diploma.

The national GED program is available for persons seventeen years or older who have not been awarded a high-school diploma. Local information about GED classes can be obtained from any high school. The program offers classes in English, social studies, science, reading, and mathematics. These classes prepare students for testing ($10.00 for a five-test battery). Achievement of minimum-average standard scoring results in a state certificate of equivalency. Retesting is arranged for students who fail to meet minimum scoring.

Students who drop out of school initially feel an upsurge of optimism, freedom, and escape from the bondage of boredom. However, the competition for unskilled work has increased tremendously because of population increases, an influx into the job market of degree-holding workers unable to find employment in their specialities, and because of the influx of married women who work while raising children. Whereas productive work adds to self-esteem, unemployment soon turns optimism into isolation from society, bitterness, and questions about one's competence. As the young person is continually rejected for simple jobs, self-esteem lowers, and apathy and depression set in.

Most schooling prepares students for more schooling, rather than teaching working skills necessary to compete in the "real" world. The drop-outs drift into despair, joins groups of other "forgotten" employables, and tend to become antisocial and cynical about "the land of opportunity." Parents can warn potential drop-outs about the inevitable disappointments that await them, but the desperately bored student thinks anything must be better than feeling chained to a desk, tortured by monotonous lectures which do not relate to life.

The experience of chronic unemployment can be maturing, forcing the teenager to find practical solutions such as joining the military service with an intent to learn employable skills, enrolling in vocational or business schools, or apprenticing to artisans, skilled workers, or craftsmen.

The educational system should develop preventive programs for potential drop-outs, programs that are stimulating and provide realistic training for students who are not interested in furthering their education beyond high school. Only the community's pressure on school boards and pleas for government subsidies will wrench a change from the entrenched "standard-operating-procedures" of our educational system. Taxpayers trying to prepare for the future of their children must become involved with this increasing problem if they expect positive changes to occur.

A group of high-school students, with the help of counselors, created a peer counseling service for those contemplating leaving school. Their program succeeded in reducing the drop-out rate 50 percent:

"Our Student Council decided to do something constructive about the drop-out problem. We made posters that read 'Drop In to Room 305 (from 4 to 5) before you Drop Out.' In the beginning we spent most of our time talking to potential drop-outs about their boredom. We discovered that most of them had never learned to think in terms of options and felt the only solution to their dilemma was to leave school.

"Our ideas evolved into a four-step program which any school can follow.

Step one:

Student talks over feelings with the peer committee and is then encouraged to confer with a counselor. Parents are invited to participate in the conference. Student is encouraged to discuss expectations, interests and personal attitudes about self-determination.

Step two:

A conference will be set to meet with the drop-out committee. The student will participate in the selection of the committee which will consist of the following:

a) Student
b) Adult committee member
c) Student's counselor
d) Other interested parties (parents and friends)
e) Peer committee member

The committee meets informally and discusses the total concept of becoming a drop-out. Alternatives and options are explored.

Step three:

The student and committee decide which options will be most beneficial for the student, and submit a written plan to the principal for review and approval.

Alternatives

Change in student's schedule.

Limit or reduce the student's load.

Half-day school with on-the-job training through a cooperative program, work-experience or work-study program in the community.

Enroll in vocational school.

Private tutoring.

Participate in evening GED classes under the sponsorship of school district.

Maintain present schedule, adding extra-curricular activities.

Step four:

The drop-out committee will carry out the follow-up program.

Meet with the student to assess if the alternative selected is fulfilling the student's needs.

Continue work with student if some alternatives fail.

Have monthly meetings with the student to identify and develop intervention strategies with the home and school.

"One of the main ingredients of our success was the attention and interest we gave to the student, which removed him or her from a state of isolation," reported a member of the peer committee.

If your children's school has no program to prevent drop-outs, you can follow the guidelines described above. Parent and child can find solutions, when discussing options and involving school counselors in the decision-making process.

"Our son had always disliked school even though his grades were good. He was interested in motorcycles and couldn't relate his studies to his consuming interest. He talked about feeling useless in school, and only feeling content when classes were over and he worked part-time at a motorcycle shop. His boss agreed to hire him full-time and offered to send him to advanced motorcycle maintenance courses. He quit school, went to work full-time and was transformed into a happy person.

"We charged him a minimal amount for room and board which he gladly paid. We don't feel that the system or we failed. Our son's interests and capabilities just didn't fit into the normal structure of education. He is productive, happy with his decision, and earning a good living."

This young man fortunately had an available job when he quit school. Others who drop out of the mainstream do not make plans beforehand, hoping everything will work out.

"Our daughter quit school in her junior year. We tried explaining that she would miss her friends, jobs would be hard to find without a diploma, and mentioned our wish for her to eventually attend college. She was adamant. She hung around the house for a month, let her appearance slide, and generally acted like a sloth. Our patience ran out and we told her to either get a job, go back to school, or leave home. Neither my husband nor I were willing to support her indolence. We explained that we loved her, but we couldn't condone her aimless life. Our feeling is that everyone has to work at something or life is meaningless.

"It was as if she had been waiting for some firm pronouncements from us. She found a job as a typist which paid enough for clothes and entertainment. We allowed her three months to learn to live within a budget and then asked for room and board. The following year she left home and moved into an apartment with some friends from work. We feel disappointed in what seems to us a limited life, working in a giant corporation with no intellectual stimulation. We have dealt with our disenchantment by accepting the fact that she has her own life which has little to do with our aspirations for her or our definition of success."

Runaways

Unhappy teenagers who feel misunderstood by parents sometimes run away from home, often involving another friend.

Many young girls just get on a bus to the nearest big city and hope for the best. They often fall into the hands of pimps, who are keenly conscious of the teenager's fantasy of finding glamor and acceptance from a comforting, worldly father figure. They shower the innocent girl with gifts, affection, new clothes, and a small place of her own. She falls in love with the smooth-talking, in-control, elegant man, becomes an addict under his careful supervision, and soon works the streets as one of his girls. By the time she may have second thoughts, her fear of beatings, her addiction, lack of escape money, and shame often prevent any attempts to contact parents.

Boys who run away can also be caught up in the dangerous underground world of drugs and sex peddlers. They can be seduced into destructive behavior, further distancing them from returning home. If they make a tentative gesture, such as a phone call, parents can assure the young person that he will be welcomed home no matter what kind of deviate experiences he may have had during his absence.

"Our son ran away when he was fifteen, taking along his fourteen-year-old girlfriend," reports his parents. They confided in none of their friends and seemed to have been swallowed into the darkness. After six months both families feared we would never see them again. One night, they telephoned from San Francisco and said they were ready to come home if we would have them. They were afraid we would be too angry to accept them back, but our relief overshadowed our hurt and anger. They arrived home, eager to resume life as carefree teenagers rather than vagabonds.

"They explained that the whole venture began as an impulsive act of romantic escape which soon turned into the need to survive as they hitchhiked from Iowa to California. They always found safe places to sleep and had odd jobs to keep themselves fed. They missed the warmth and security of home but were afraid to 'face the music,' and so kept on traveling. As parents, we were blameless in that we did nothing to drive them away. They weren't running away from us, but toward excitement and adventure. We don't really forgive their inconsiderateness, nor have we recovered from the anxiety and worry they caused us, but we are glad to have our son back in one piece. He promises never to act so unwisely again."

Because there are so many runaways each year, the police are unable to be of much assistance. Not very many people can afford the services of a detective agency. Most parents wait and hope for the best while suffering guilt over what they did wrong (sometimes nothing), tortured by worry and fears for their children's lives.

Some teenagers leave to "find themselves" without having shown any symptoms of restlessness before the disappearance—the most shocking kind of runaway experience for parents. Seemingly happy-go-lucky teenagers may be wearing a socially approved mask, while feeling miserable, alone, and different. They may think the solution to their normal living problems is to leave the known and start fresh in some new, exotic surroundings. Having a "happy" child run away is of course less likely to happen if parents are in tune and talking with their growing children.

In the face of sorrow over a runaway, parents will feel some comfort if they share their worries with each other and the children remaining in the home. Brothers and sisters will feel confused and frightened by an older sibling's disappearance and will need emotional support, too. Surprisingly, they often rally around their parents and are helpful to the adults. However, underneath the concern and anxiety, all members of the family feel angry when a teenager takes off with no consideration for family feelings. The anger is normal and should be aired along with feelings of guilt and anxiety.

When and if a runaway calls for help and wants to return home, he or she will most likely feel ashamed, undeserving of family love, and disgusted with themselves over some experiences. The entire family is wounded and traumatized by the disappearing teenager, the time spent worrying, and the stress of the reunion. A returned child may not want to talk about his or her adventures for quite some time, and persistent questioning may only cause withdrawal. If a family accepts a runaway back into the home, it must do so expecting to give support rather than to receive apologies—at least in the beginning. Patience and the availability of understanding parents will eventually relax teenagers enough for them to share their reasons for unhappiness.

Unexpected Pregnancy

During the last ten or fifteen years many people have experienced the surprise of some "nice" girl in the community announcing her pregnancy. It is always a shock to parents to discover that their attempts at sex education have been ignored. We must keep in mind that many women in the past generations also became pregnant, but the solution was usually to arrange a quick wedding, and then, seven months later, to announce the birth of a premature baby to the relatives. Today's young people, with many plans for the future, do not consider that rushing to the altar at sixteen or seventeen is a very wise move.

Girls who suspect they may be pregnant usually suffer alone during the first month after a missed menstrual period. When pregnancy can no longer be denied, they must discuss the problem with their parents. A pregnant daughter may feel worry that her parents will be angry and rejecting, embarrassed by her lack of birth control, or confused and upset if her boyfriend has swiftly dropped her after an announcement of pregnancy. She needs parents' emotional support, guidance, and assurance of love more than any other time of her life. She already knows she has made a big mistake, and therefore inducing guilt or harsh recriminations solve nothing.

The question of abortion must be decided after a visit to the doctor to determine the age of the fetus. Abortion is not traumatic for the patient when handled with kindness by parents and the hospital staff. Depending on the degree of her emotional involvement with her sexual partner and her feeling about destroying a potential life, the girl may experience some guilt and enter into a period of mourning. Avoiding these feelings leads to vague physical complaints and future depression that cannot be pinpointed. Giving the aborting girl an opportunity to cry and talk about her feelings with parents or friends is far better.

We have seen many young adults who had abortions in their teen years take the matter so casually that the memory is minor and undisturbing. They comment that so many of their friends went through the same thing that it didn't seem to be a big deal as long as their parents were helpful.

"One night at the dinner table, our sixteen-year-old, Chris, gravely announced she was pregnant. Before we could react, she listed her plans for abortion and plans to pay for medical expenses. She turned to her father and asked if he would want her to leave home. He was stunned that she expected a rejection from him. He enveloped her in his arms and said, 'Loving you doesn't stop because you made a mistake. We'll live through this together.' They argued about her boyfriend's responsibility, and Chris wanted to leave him entirely out of the matter. She hadn't told him about her pregnancy. My husband accused her of being sexist to take the entire blame and said that her boyfriend should share in the cost and emotional experience. She was naturally afraid that he would abandon her. We suggested that he deserved a chance to prove his character.

"The knowledge of our support gave Chris the courage to tell her boyfriend. They had a conference in her room and, when finished, joined us in the kitchen. He was embarrassed, but very manly, offering to pay for half the expenses. They both agreed to keep the matter an official secret from friends and his relatives. He said, 'My parents would not be understanding. I'd rather handle this myself. Chris and I may not be ready for marriage, but we still love each other.'

"The four of us lived through the abortion and life went on normally. The children's obvious sexual activity gave us the right to insist on birth control for Chris. We are very glad she came directly to us and that we insisted she involve her boyfriend in the crisis. They eventually broke up but remain friends."

Some families, because of religious or ethical principles, consider abortion out of the question. Some religious and ethnic groups accept illegitimate children into the family attaching no stigma to the mother or child, absorbing the infant into the extending family.

The girl who insists that she wants to keep the baby usually has no idea what the future entails. Parents should not be expected to support a new child after all the years of expense and care connected with their own offspring. A wise obstetrician friend of ours listens sympathetically to the feelings of girls wanting to face the world alone with their babies by their side. He recognizes that hidden beneath the wish to keep the baby is the fantasy that the baby will love them and make up for all the unpleasantness of adolescence.

The doctor has an arrangement with mothers who have small infants at home. He sets up a visit at the home of the newborn and asks the pregnant girl to spend at least two days and nights helping out with the infant. The introduction to the reality of baby care—an infant's persistent and insistent needs for feeding, cleaning, and affection—usually opens up the eyes of the idealistic youngster. The girl usually can come to understand that her baby will be welcomed into the home of parents who can maturely care for its needs, and usually agrees to give the baby up for adoption.

"Our daughter decided she wanted to keep her child and hoped we would let her stay home. She felt a spiritual need to be a mother and even though she was just seventeen, felt she would be a responsible parent. She quit high school, remaining at home, and took over all the household duties. We accepted her decision and loved her just as we always had. When her daughter was born, I took a couple of weeks' vacation time and helped her care for our new family member. Our friends and relatives celebrated the birth of our grandchild with us. We expected their acceptance and they didn't disappoint us. Our daughter graduated from high school by attending night school. When her daughter was two she went to work to support them and paid back all the expenses incurred during pregnancy and her daughter's infancy. We enjoyed our granddaughter and we all grew closer as my husband, myself and daughter shared baby and child care responsibilities. Last year, she married a wonderful man who didn't think it important that his new little girl began life with just one parent."

Everyone makes mistakes during a lifetime, and pregnancy is just more physically evident than most errors. Forget worrying about what neighbors or relatives will say about her or your family. The most important issue is giving emotional support and then moving on in life.

Drugs

All teenagers must make decisions about drugs, from tobacco to PCB. Children are offered drugs as early as grade school, and most teenagers have experimented with some. When teenagers ask parents' opinions about drug use, they are often trying to elicit a set of standards from adults. To tell an adolescent, "These decisions are up to you" can leave the person floundering. If teenagers ask about drugs, parents should familiarize themselves with the effects of drugs on the body, share the information, and clearly state their preferences about drug usage. Some children are afraid to try drugs and seek parental support to buttress them from temptation. Some parents smoke marijuana as a matter of course, and have no qualms about their offspring doing the same. Most children have seen their parents drinking alcohol, as it is the usual ingredient for socializing in our society.

The Urge to Experiment

Responsible parenting requires honest discussions about drug use. Drug experimentation is a subject that must be open for debate, just as any other pertinent subject today's teenagers must decide upon. Educating teenagers about drugs will not automatically inspire them to try everything.

Teenagers should be advised that using any drug involves personal responsibilities. If drugs are used as an escape from life rather than as an enhancement of good feelings, drugs will perpetuate problems. Learning to handle tension, conflicts and challenges, is a normal part of living. Using drugs to blot out every hassle is escapism. The person who drives after drinking courts disaster. Smoking is pleasurable but has unhealthy side effects. Taking hallucinogens can be dangerous. Tranquilizers are addicting.

The majority of drugs tend to isolate a person rather than stimulating involvement with others. Young people will experiment with drugs and discover whether they add to or diminish pleasure.

The Current Drug Scene

Uppers

Amphetamines lift the mood, speed up thought processes, increase physical energy, induce quickening of speech, and heighten sensory awareness. Also known as "speed," amphetamines are available in several forms: Dexedrine, Benzedrine or "bennies," and diet pills. Cocaine is an upper which is often sniffed through the nose.

Downers

Barbiturates are drugs such as Nembutal, Seconal, or sleeping pills found in medicine cabinets of many homes. They are sedatives which induce drowsiness and sleep. They may be physically addicting and are extremely dangerous when combined with alcohol.

Tranquilizers

Tranquilizers reduce excessive anxiety and are readily available in most homes.

Angel Dust is a monkey and horse tranquilizer which has been described as an ultimate death trip since large numbers of teenagers have died from overdoses of PCP, also known as rocket fuel, and crystal. It comes in the form of dust which is sprinkled on cigarettes.

Narcotics

Most narcotics are derivatives of the opium poppy. Narcotics relieve pain and induce sleep. Heroin is the strongest illegal drug, also known as "junk," "snow," "horse," "stuff," and "H." An injection of heroin produces a relaxed, high pleasurable, dreamlike state. The body becomes addicted to heroin, requiring increasing amounts to maintain a high and avoid the extremely unpleasant withdrawal symptoms.

Hallucinogenic Drugs

These drugs alter the consciousness of the mind, causing a distortion of reality either visually, auditorally, or in taste. Marijuana induces a dreamlike, passive state of pleasure wherein nothing seems of great significance. Mescaline from the peyote cactus, psilocybin from the Mexican mushroom, and the most powerful LSD or lysergic acid, alter the user's perception of reality. Depending upon the person's emotional stability, the environment and the dosage, a LSD trip can range from pleasant imagery and accompanying delightful feelings to enormous dread and panic.

Experimentation does not necessarily lead to drug abuse. A drug abuser is a person who uses drugs excessively as a crutch to avoid reality. There are no accurate lists of symptoms to define a drug abuser. You have known your children all their lives. Even though mood fluctuations are common in teenagers, everyone has unique modes of behavior and predictable mannerisms. If your teenager deviates strangely from usual behavior, acting bizarre or weird, something is wrong. It may be a drug-related problem, and the only common-sense approach is to ask your child if he or she is using drugs. Any erratic change in behavior should alert parents to the possibility of problems.

Drugs are expensive. You have the right to inquire where your teenager acquires the money to pay for expensive drugs. A decision must be reached if you discover your teenager sells drugs. A person who refuses to abide by family rules and opts for criminal activity should be given two options: quit and work with parents or a therapist to overcome antisocial behavior or leave home. Before this drastic step becomes a reality, signs of impending problems should be obvious, and should be handled.

Drugs are available everywhere. Preventing drug abuse rests with parental education, conversation, and helping young people learn to cope with living problems with inner resources, instead of escaping into the dream world of chemical happiness.

A teenager who is arrested in a drug bust finds the experience so unpleasant and demeaning that he or she usually avoids drug parties in the future. Parents need a lawyer to help them through the court system if a teenager is brought to trial. As with other expenses incurred when teenagers break the law, they should pay back their parents' expenditures for attorney fees and court costs.

Alcohol

The last ten years have seen an enormous increase in alcohol consumption by teenagers. Alcohol addiction is common and is directly related to many teenage car accidents and vehicular deaths. Several years ago, Dr. Morris E. Chafetz of the National Institute of Alcohol Abuse and Alcoholism stated, "By every measurement, alcohol is *the* drug causing the greatest number of serious problems among young people."

Teenagers witness parents drinking. Since alcohol is not an illegal drug, parents often accept teenage drinking as well. Also, alcohol was the drug of their own choice when they were adolescents and has remained so. Whereas many other drugs tend to cause withdrawal into the self, alcohol makes everyone more gregarious. As most teenagers suffer from shyness, alcohol lubricates their tongues and makes socializing much easier—just as they have seen it do at adult parties.

The ability to "hold your liquor" has always been associated with manliness in our society. In many states the ability to buy alcohol legally is a rite of passage into adulthood, even more important than the euphoria connected with earning one's first driver's license.

Young people should be educated in how alcohol affects behavior. Alcohol is called a depressant drug. Many teenagers are confused by this label since drinking doesn't seem to make them moody or sad. What alcohol depresses is a person's sense of right and wrong, anesthetizing the part of the brain that makes choices and decides what is correct. For this reason drunks insist on driving when they can barely walk, steal when they would usually be honest, and even commit murder. Alcohol removes the sensitive checks and balances that humans employ in all decisions.

Parents can discuss these matters and point out that the great majority of heavy drinkers drink only to get drunk, instead of wishing to enjoy a pleasant glow. Getting blitzed covers up fears of being oneself or relating warmly and genuinely to others—and eventually increases loneliness.

A friend of ours related how one day her teenage son and daughter came home intoxicated and sick to their stomachs. She held their heads as they vomited to the stage of dry heaves, washed their faces, dried their tears, and listened to their promises: "I'll never, ever do this to myself again." Knowing they would be groggy and hung over the next morning, the mother thought that this experience would teach them a lesson. To her amazement, her teenagers' youthful physical constitutions healed them during the night, and they woke up feeling fine, alert, and without the usual symptoms of a hangover. They did feel sheepish about the scene they had made but had amnesia about most of their moaning and groanings. The mother said, "You both drank too much, too fast, and got too sick. If you can't use moderation, don't expect me to be your nurse again. Once is enough!" She then asked them, in a matter-of-fact tone, what they would think of her if she came home falling into things, vomiting, and needing care. They were horrified but got the point: if they insisted on using an adult drug, they should be prepared to handle it with maturity.

Calmly turning the tables on teenagers is an effective technique that teaches them to think about another side of an issue and to use empathy and consideration. The technique is most effective when applied through casual questioning rather than by reproachful or guilt-inducing comments ("How can you do this to me!"). Teenagers enjoy thinking up hypothetical questions and answers, and asking them to walk in another's shoes presents them with a challenge. Of course, they, in turn, have the right to ask us to imagine ourselves as them.

As parents discuss drinking with their teenagers, they can explain that young people have the right to be courageous and say "no" when pressured to drink. They should have enough respect for their lives to refuse to be passengers in cars with drunk drivers. Most parents would rather get up in the middle of the night to pick up stranded children than to have them take chances with drunk drivers. If a driving teenager drinks too much at a party, he or she can stay the night with friends or allow a sober person to give a lift home. When teenagers hear such commonsense approaches enough, the rules will become, hopefully, automatic.

Unilaterally forbidding any experimentation with drugs makes them too fascinating. The normal, rebellious, spunky adolescent will take this taboo as an invitation to try drugs. Giving reasonable and educational guidelines, presented with the welfare of the young in mind, is a better approach than demanding total obedience.

Parents are the best example to teenagers, who observe and imitate. If children witness drunk parents, or parents who automatically consume tranquilizers to "get through the day," they will turn a deaf ear on "do what I say, not what I do" admonitions.

Suicide

Parents are devastated when their beloved children attempt suicide or succeed in killing themselves. Disbelief, confusion, guilt, and anger prevail when a young person sinks to the depths of despair which culminates in self-extermination. Suicide attempts include the use of weapons, overdoses of drugs, car crashes, or living life as dangerously as possible, courting death. Previously discussed, anorexia nervosa is a passive form of suicide through self-induced starvation.

Teenagers, with their heightened sense of drama and their self-preoccupation, often view suicide as a glamorous and theatrical possibility. Adolescents frequently deal with problems by acting out their feelings, such as stealing, vandalism, or drug abuse as an outlet for anger. Suicide is the ultimate form of acting out aggression against the self or others.

Adults clearly understand that death is irreversible. Teenagers often have the fantasy that they can "kill" themselves but not really die—a form of magical thinking left over from childhood. Rescued suicidal teenagers often claim thinking they would be present after death to witness everyone's sorrow.

Thoughts of suicide can occur when a teenager is rejected by a loved one, feels imprisoned by parental misunderstanding or harsh rules, depressed over pressures of daily frustrations, or feels that there is no solution to a personal crisis. They don't want to actually die, but just feel life is not worth living with what they perceive as continual suffering. Adults' experience teaches that crises are resolvable, as time and energies invested in problems create change, results, or adjustment to loss. Teenagers who may feel isolated from family and friends, who are experiencing failure in school or relationships, can comprehend no such long-term solutions to their crushing burdens. The comforting, nondemanding state of death becomes the ultimate appealing answer to an overwhelming sense of powerlessness to control life events.

The alarming aspect of many teenage suicides is the obviously impulsive nature of the decision and consequent act. Adults often contemplate, plan, write notes, or seek help from suicide hot lines or professionals before actually making a suicide gesture. Teenagers act impulsively by nature. Coupled with their fantasy of continued life after suicide, spontaneous acts of self-destruction frequently happen, fueled by low self-esteem and an omnipotent courageous resolve to meet death head first. Impulsive actions which result in death cannot be blamed on parents, friends, or professionals who may be treating a suicide-prone adolescent. These incidents often transpire so quickly that even people alert to the possibility have no opportunity for rescue.

Because even normal adolescents can suddenly become suicidal when deeply depressed or faced with a complex crisis, homes should not contain available weapons or large quantities of potentially lethal drugs. Just as parents kept dangerous household chemicals out of the reach of toddlers, destructive objects should be kept in a secure place when living with teenagers.

Preventive measures against suicide are keeping in touch with teen-agers' emotional state by free-flowing communication in the home, and teaching the growing person about options to problem solving.

Depressed teenagers need to talk about their feelings of despair which may originate from rejection, failure, social stresses, or psycho-logical isolation from society (no one cares or understands).

The symptoms of depression can be a pervasive dread uncon-nected to reality, fatigue with accompanying feelings of physical heaviness, insomnia, inability to concentrate, changes in appetite, tearfulness, feeling persecuted and helpless. Many teenagers suffer these feelings during the psychological upheaval of adolescence. When the symptoms persist, professional help is indicated to help ward off a possible suicide attempt. Therapists attempt to delve beneath the feelings of depression and uncover the anger toward the self or others which causes despair. The patient often denies anger and cannot confront rage without the support and guidance of a therapist. The goal of treatment is to teach the teenager to accept negative feelings, learn to solve problems with intellectual skills rather than emotional forces, discover inner resources, develop self-confi-dence, and discover that it takes more courage to live than to die.

Cries for help from a pre-suicidal adolescent can be talking about the wish to die, wrist-slashing, pill-gulping, or continual involvement in dangerous death-defying activities. Sometimes a teenager who has been agitated will suddenly become serene, and give away precious possessions as a prelude to quietly committing suicide as the ultimate answer to problems. All these signals are serious warnings of ruminations about self-destruction and help should be sought as quickly as possible.

The suicide-prone or attempted-suicider should be treated as any other ill person. They require patience, emotional support, and non-demanding companionship. The anger and disgust over the stupidity of suicide that parents and relatives often feel can be discussed together, with friends or a therapist. These reactions are normal responses to the infantile behavior of suicidal people, but cannot be exposed to the patient during recovery and treatment.

Expecting Trouble

Dealing with mid-adolescent acts of aggression, whether directed toward themselves or others, is easier to handle when parents expect that some trouble will occur in these years of learning self-control. The adolescent years are rarely smooth, and if they were, the young people would never develop the experience and coping skills necessary to confront the problems which they will face as adults. Parents stumble out of the adolescent years with graying hair and sighs of relief as their teenagers begin to mature and stabilize.

SEVEN

The Unbridged Gulf

Parents have often confided, after children leave home, that the teen years put the most stress on their marriage. They suddenly found themselves opposing each other's methods of adolescent management, after years of agreement on how to deal with little children.

The Battle of Dirt

Sixteen-year-old Paul flops into a living room chair. His hair is greasy, and his face and hands grimy. He gulps down two huge sandwiches, unaware of the crumbs drifting like snowflakes onto the floor and furniture. He lurches up, tripping over a coffee table, hulks into the kitchen to grab some cookies, and plunks himself down again. He loudly complains of a sudden ache in his side. Paul's mother, irritated by his slothful appearance and messy eating habits, knows if she nags he will defiantly refuse to clean up his act. She says, "You know, sudden pains like that can be caused when people forget to take showers. The dirt kind of seeps into the bod and collects in one spot." Paul, not knowing whether or not to believe this bit of made-up medical information, glances suspiciously at his mother. She maintains a cheerful attitude and goes about her affairs. Ten minutes later, her son is in the shower vigorously scrubbing and shampooing. She makes no comment when he reenters the living room. He asks for the car keys, and she says, "Sure you can, after you vacuum the chair and the rug where you just ate." He does the small job and gets the car.

Paul, now a man, had this story recounted to him by his mother. He had no memory of it but laughed heartily about his mother's clever manipulations. He also felt embarrassed about his old teenage grossness. His mother's opinion had been that a creative lie was the most effective weapon for getting her messy son to take a shower. Remembering those days, she says, "You know, dirt can be sullen when it's attached to a teenager. Teenagers wear it like a chip on their shoulder, taking pleasure in parents' disgust. I refused to play into the 'give command-receive sullen defiance' game, so I invented my own methods."

Her husband, however, had thought that her maneuvers were a waste of time. For a month at a time, he didn't say more than five words to his son. Whenever he saw Paul, he told him to leave the room, clean up, or comb his hair. Every time the man looked at his son, he felt irritated and angry. The boy sulked away and never complied with his father's demands. Father and son handled their animosity by avoiding each other. The husband blamed his wife for their child's adolescent romance with dirt. She, in turn, thought he was cruel and rejecting. Since they all lived in the same house, everyone felt misunderstood, strained, and uneasy.

Paul secretly enjoyed the rift he was causing between his parents. He became even more messy in appearance, adding fuel to the flames. His father was a fastidiously clean person, and the son's normal teenage sloppiness became the symbol of his rebellion against his father's influence.

The mother tried to talk with her son and husband, but they were too fiercely locked into a battle of hate. Finally, Paul left home and went to live with a friend. When he arrived at the supper table on the first day at his pal's house, the father of the house said, "The rule around here is: only clean people get to eat my food, which comes from my hard-earned paycheck." He was a confident, self-assured person and felt that anyone who enjoyed his food should abide by his rules. "It's my house," he explained, "and kids respect you if you're firm about practical matters. I don't like to look at dirty people, and I don't care if they're going through some phase or other." His direct, no-nonsense approach worked perfectly.

In the meantime, Paul's parents continued to fight even while their son was absent, the mother accusing the father of forcing their only child out of the house, and the father accusing her of spoiling her little baby boy.

Their son returned after three weeks, cleaned up his room, and, much to his parents' amazement, was himself clean in body. He had learned a great deal from his pal's father—a man who was objective, intelligent, straightforward, and uninvolved in the family battle. As often happens, a sullen, angry teenager will listen to another adult, untinged in that relationship by the ambivalence connected with parents.

Paul asked for a family conference and, with a new confidence, admitted that he was to blame for causing such a rift in the family. He shared with his father that he had used the device of sullen dirt to get attention; even negative attention had felt better than being ignored. He told his mother that as long as she was soft on him, he would normally take advantage of her. His friend's father had suggested that instead of acting out angry feelings by flaunting dirt and grime, he should initiate a frank talk with his family. "He got me to see that we would just keep hating each other if I didn't stop playing games with the two of you. He also made me feel dumb and like a little kid to be getting a kick out of torturing both of you."

At first his father felt inferior because someone else could effect such a drastic change in his son—after his own yelling and swearing had been ignored. He next felt grateful that another person took the time to talk sensibly to his boy. Then he felt proud for his son's courage to admit his motivations and talk to them so maturely.

They became a family again as each spoke honestly about his or her feelings. The mother learned that her permissive approach and sly manipulations only subtly encouraged his indulgence in sloppiness. "I don't want to be in the middle of you two anymore. From now on if you talk things over, the three of us can enjoy living together again." The father recognized that he had spent little time paying positive attention to his son, only dealing out critical comments about his appearance. He also admitted that he felt some jealousy toward the boy because he had so much freedom, unlike his own boyhood when he had to work to help support his family. "I guess we all took out our feelings in the area of dirt, instead of being aware of what was brewing underneath."

During the next few years the family still had arguments and disagreements, but they learned to figure out their angers instead of getting stuck in the "parental demand–adolescent defiance" game.

A Break from Parents

Sometimes, the battle becomes so entrenched that neither child nor parent wants to give in, clear the air, or try something new.

Judy and her single mother had been at odds for three years. Her mother supported her and Judy's two brothers with minimal financial aid from her long-divorced husband. He had remarried, and he visited the children rarely.

Judy had responsibilities that included keeping track of her rambunctious brothers, cleaning the house, and getting dinner started before her mother came home from work. It seemed to Judy that no matter how much she accomplished, her mother was never satisfied. They had constant, bickering conversations which lasted throughout the evening, usually culminating in Judy's slamming off to her room.

Her mother, worn out from a demanding job, was irritated when she arrived home and she automatically took out her work frustrations on her daughter. She was a perfectionist and couldn't understand why Judy wasn't neat and tidy like herself. She had no awareness that teenagers sometimes need to adopt habits opposite from their parents' in order to declare their individuality. If mother had been a casual housekeeper, then daughter probably would have been superneat—nothing personal, just a sign of declaring one's individuality.

As Judy grew older, more verbal, and increasingly angry at her mother's critical attitude, she refused to do anything helpful. She ignored her brothers, letting them tear up the house, "forgot" to start dinner, and talked on the phone with her boyfriend. He was another bone of contention. Judy thought his dark looks glamorous. Mother thought he looked, dressed, and acted like a gangster, and refused to allow him into the house. The home vibrated with hostilities.

At the suggestion of a concerned friend, Judy's mother sent her to spend the summer with her father. Judy became a happier person, released from the tension at home and the constant bickering with her mother. She enjoyed the status of being an only child with her father and stepmother. Her brothers missed her and accused their mother of deliberately sending Judy away. They ignored her instructions to behave. Mother felt miserably alone and unable to discipline her two wild boys. She also came to realize how much she had depended on Judy's help. When it was time for Judy to return home, Judy asked to remain with her father. The boys insisted that they, too, should have a chance to be with their father.

After much thought and many conferences with her ex-mate, the mother decided to let her children go. "I admitted to myself that I couldn't control three teenagers. They needed a father *and* a mother. I did fine when they were little, but I'm too set in my ways to be understanding about teenagers. At first, I felt like a failure and that the kids didn't appreciate me or love me, but then friends helped me to see that the children had a right to choose. Their choice didn't have anything to do with appreciation or love. I'm grateful to their step-mother. She likes teenagers and has a knack with them. I feel I did my share of raising our children, so now it's their father's turn." She is the visiting parent now, and enjoys her freedom and also her children.

Parents should not feel that they have failed if life becomes better for all when a teenager opts to live elsewhere—for a week, a month, or years. If families make realistic living arrangements, they may save their future relationships. We know of two families who swap their teenagers during the summer, even if nothing is wrong. They think it's a good experience for everyone to learn to live with others. The five children involved all like it too, and are relieved to get a break from their parents.

To consider letting a teenager live with a divorced mate or with friends or relatives is not giving up. Parents who find themselves disliking their rebellious teenagers should accept the condition as normal: no one loves or even likes his or her children all the time. A vacation from the war of nerves can be beneficial to everyone.

Withdrawing from the Problem

A father told us that he was disgusted with his two teenage girls, who were both extremely bright, gifted musicians and quite attractive. When they were fourteen and fifteen, they spent their time refuting all of his opinions, lost interest in their music, and made up a secret language which he assumed was directed at making fun of him. "If you think teenage boys are slobs, you should have seen my girls' disasters, which they called the bathroom and bedroom."

What confused the father was that whenever he met other adults who knew his daughters, they were full of praise for his girls. "I thought they were discussing strangers when people spoke of their poise, sense of humor, and initiative. I never tried to learn about their good side because I was so angry at what I assumed were personal attacks on me. I finally withdrew from them, and I'm sorry for it now. They've married and moved away, and seldom visit."

We suggested that now that the daughters were adults, perhaps the rift could be bridged. Why not admit to them he just didn't understand their adolescent ways and honestly admit regret? This option had never occurred to him, and he did write—a rather elaborate, intellectualized version of his remorse. His elder daughter responded warmly and suggested that the folks come to visit her home in California. "Perhaps we can get closer on my turf, without all those old, hostile memories in your house." The reunion was strained at first, but eventually everyone relaxed, since the motivations were healthy and honest. A rebonding took place, after a ten-year drought of feelings. They all admitted how much they had hated each other in the past, but were now meeting on an adult level, attempting a different kind of emotional connection. The mother was relieved, for she had held a grudge against her husband for abandoning the girls during their adolescence. And the father was optimistic: "One day, my youngest will also get over her stubborn stance about my being a son-of-a-bitch, but right now I feel like a loving and loved father again."

Comparisons with a Dead Sibling

A problem that plagues some families is comparing a child in the family to a dead sibling. Parents, in their grief and guilt over a child's death, will imagine an idealized personality for the lost child. The remaining children can never match up to the fantasized behavior of the dead relative.

Parents who unwittingly compare their dead child with a normally floundering teenager will say, "Oh, our Johnny wouldn't have been so cross, slobby, clumsy, melodramatic, and irresponsible as you. Why can't you act more mature, like your brother would have?" This makes the real-life teenager jealous of the idealized dead son, which in turn causes guilt over negative feelings for a lost brother. The normally sloppy or rebellious child feels a deep frustration, since he or she knows that being judged against an unrealistically idealized image of a teenager is unfair.

The death of a child is unbearable and unlike any other sorrow parents will experience. They have been abruptly robbed of the young person's potential. All the love and care lavished on the child never reaches any fruition or harvest. The loss is felt daily, and most parents feel guilty, thinking they could have prevented their child's death. Many times parents do not ever recover from the loss of a child, but they should allow their other children to lead normal lives without comparisons to dead siblings, and should not expect them to grieve as deeply as they do.

Parents have not completed mourning when they keep a child's memory alive by investing him or her with idealized personality traits as if life had continued. It is healthier to remember and talk about the actual life of the child rather than imaginary characteristics. Other family members can relate to the lost child's actual life history without feeling they must compete with a fantasy figure.

Sometimes the help of a therapist is needed to bring about understanding in cases of prolonged mourning.

Parental Possessiveness

Another stress on marriage and family relations occurs when one parent becomes too possessive of a teenage child. Possessiveness is not love, although the parent may think it is. Wanting to remain the child's first love priority is unrealistic and stifling to emotional growth. Possessively clinging to a child always ends up in the offspring's escape.

Ann, a woman in her fifties, is still mystified over her twenty-year-old son's lack of warmth. She pleads with Lance to come home for holidays, insisting that such visits are his duty to his family, but he always has some important or urgent business which keeps him away.

Ann had three children—two girls and a boy. The mother's favorite had always been Lance. She had unconsciously kept a rivalry going between the children in order to keep them separated. When her son was a youngster, he really liked being treated as a prince, always lording it over his sisters when the mother took his side. He got away with murder. But his mother's great love for him became an embarrassment when he first fell in love.

"She was just a sweet little girl, about thirteen," Lance recalls his first love. "I was fourteen and crazy about her. You would have thought we were going to get married the way my mom carried on. She talked about the girl like she was some kind of evil person. It was awful. It was about then that I started to get the inkling that my mother was, ugh, like, in love with me, instead of loving me like mothers are supposed to.

"It didn't feel exactly sexual, but like I belonged to her. Everything I did was overpraised and exaggerated to the point where I felt uncomfortable. My dad was never home much, out making money, I guess. My sisters hated me. I would have, too—after watching someone else get the royal treatment all those years. I became mostly silent at home, trying to remove myself from mother. I wanted to shriek and run away whenever she'd want to kiss me or touch my hair, always with adoring eyes.

"When it was time for high school, I demanded that my father send me away to boarding school. Since I always got my own way, they sent me to a school in the West. I loved it and was bugged by only one thing—too many letters from mom. I've suffered with friends and lovers, though. When a parent spoils you with too much gooey love and makes you a favorite, you begin to think other people should treat you like that, too. I'm still learning that lesson. My mother hasn't learned anything. I often wonder if my father knew what was going on, but I doubt it. He only says, 'Please come home for your mother's sake.' I haven't been there for two years, and it'll be a while before I can handle her without feeling weird. I've met a couple of other people with possessive parents, and they feel the same as I do."

If you find yourself too attached to one child, always taking his or her side, being overly protective, or being jealous when other people begin to replace you, consider your reasons for feeling this way. If a spouse is too possessive with one of the children, question him or her in a nonthreatening manner. Children who are unconditionally loved and adored beyond the infant years do not develop a realistic view of themselves or the world. As they grow older they resent the unearned glorification and will quickly distance themselves from suffocating parents.

If a parent turns to a child for love gratification, the parent disrupts the normal generational boundaries, turning the child into a miniature spouse. Often the insight that a parent is having an unconscious romance with a child is sufficient to correct behavior. If talking about feelings with an objective, helpful mate or with friends does not relieve the possessive feelings, therapy should be considered.

Too Wide a Gulf

Perhaps you find yourself in an unworkable, vicious circle in which you, your spouse, and your teenage children continue to wage war with no solutions in sight. An objective third party should then be consulted. Family therapy is usually effective in sorting out problems and making everyone take responsibility for his or her part in the strife. Sometimes, families become so involved in complex struggles for control versus independence that only a professional can find an equitable solution. Seeking professional help can certainly be worth the time and effort in order to achieve family harmony.

EIGHT

The Single Parent

Teenagers and Divorce

Adolescents are accustomed to divorce as a pervasive social ailment, but assume their families will be immune.

During divorce, family bonds that teenagers detach at their own pace are suddenly wrenched apart, leaving them with additional psychological burdens. Teenagers resent adult problems which disrupt their lives, naturally preferring intact family security for their journey toward individuation.

A group of teenagers meet at our clinic to discuss their feelings about divorce. All of them have recently suffered the loss of a parent. These are some of their comments.

"I really felt pissed off. My parents were always so quiet, you know. One day my dad comes into my room—instant anxiety—and tells me he's leaving. Just like that. No warning. It would have been easier if I knew what was coming down."

"It really makes you feel unimportant to them. Here these two adults decide your future and don't even consult you."

"I'm embarrassed to tell my friends about my folks' split. I make up excuses when someone wants to come over. I just pretend everything's cool."

141

"My mother just disappeared one day. She didn't even leave a note. How's that for being a loving mother?"

"I feel like it's the death of my family. My mom drinks in the kitchen, my little sister cries all the time, and I feel blank."

These teenagers get a chance to vent the angry and helpless feelings which are always present when parents divorce. The main thread which runs through their unhappiness is that parents hid the truth from them. They wanted to be included in talks about separation instead of having the news dropped on them, and feel adjustments would have been easier if they had at least been consulted, even if they couldn't influence their parents' final actions.

"My parents fought constantly. When they finally divorced, I wasn't surprised," says fifteen-year-old John. "The noise level sure went down at our house, but I felt confused. Their fights centered on trivia, with no really big problem to help me understand why they hated each other. They're too touchy to answer any questions about the real reason for their split. They're always using me as a go-between, and I feel pulled between two people who are supposed to be adults."

If parents can be specific, teenagers need to know the reasons for parental separation, seeking reassurance that they are not to blame. Divorce affects their futures, and, in fairness, they should be given thorough explanations by both parents. Young people prefer the truth, often displaying empathy and understanding after honest discussions.

"My folks called a family conference. My sister and I groaned and dragged our feet to the meeting, knowing we would have to listen to complaints about our teenage slobbery. We slumped down on the couch, waiting for a lecture. Dad started with such a soft voice that Dena and I jerked our heads up. He was crying and so was Mom. We started to cry too, reacting to their sadness. Like in some foreign movie everyone fell into a huddle, hugging and weeping. They held us close and said they were getting a divorce. In unison Dena and I asked, 'why?' Dad explained they had no man-woman love feelings, and existed in their marriage like a brother and sister. 'It's easy to live without fighting, but life isn't very joyous. I've fallen in love with someone else, and your mother has gracefully agreed to end our marriage. I've discovered romantic love is vital to me.'

"It seemed crazy that he was talking about love. I didn't believe old people needed romance, and I told him he was selfish. He agreed that he was thinking of his own well-being but promised he would always be around as a friend and father. Mom was calm and said, 'Everyone's selfish. You probably want everything to stay the same for your comfort. At first, I wanted to balk, fearing change. Should I be more selfish than your father and demand he stay when he doesn't love me except as an old friend? You'll both be leaving home soon. Should he live for your convenience? You don't have to like our decision, but we'll all survive.'

"We muddled through, mostly because our parents listened to our feelings, and they stayed friends. We didn't feel pulled between them. I'm twenty now and still have memories of that dramatic family conference. As a normal teenager, my concerns were self-centered. I later came to understand that my father actually felt as if he were dying without passion in his life. Their honesty helped Dena and me really understand that we didn't cause their unhappiness."

The Divorced Mother

Women usually receive custody of the children. The everyday problems of living with teenagers can loom as overwhelming, and one is lonely without another adult to share the load.

"My shift to single parenthood was abrupt. My marriage was never great, but seemed bearable. My husband left one morning, leaving a typewritten note saying he was seeking a divorce, traveling on business, and directing me to his attorney who was informed and prepared to write checks for the family's support. He ended twenty years of marriage like a sterile business deal.

"I was shocked and felt helpless, but my anger saw me through the worst days. I refused to collapse over such a bastard. I did some crying with friends and then told the kids the news. They hadn't suspected anything as my husband was often away on business trips, and they are all normally active and busy with their own friends and activities. My sons, thirteen, sixteen, and eighteen, were furious because, in their eyes, their father had acted in a cowardly way by not telling us in person. He did write to them individually and explained he would discuss the divorce with them—which was more than he did for me.

"I had to face priorities, the first one being an evaluation of my family roles. I told my sons that I was not going to try to be a mother and a father, just mother, and that their father would continue to be a responsible parent. I insisted that none of them consider himself the man of the house, but be themselves. I explained that I would keep working, money was provided for essentials, our home would remain the same, but they would need to find part-time jobs for extras.

"My next priority was to get them to talk about their anger. This was easy because they felt deserted, and were eager to pour out their vituperate thoughts on the disappearance.

"It's been three years since my divorce. My ex-mate arranged to visit the boys as soon as he returned, and they felt loved again. I understand that children are attached to both parents and have never asked my sons to reject their father because he treated me badly. Besides, I am happier since he left and freed me from marital stress.

"My oldest was fairly independent from parenting needs and soon left for college. He thrashed out his negative feelings with his father and usually stays with him when he's home from school.

"Sixteen-year-old Greg became verbally abusive with me for 'not keeping Dad happy.' I was unprepared for his hostility and became defensive. Gradually, I learned to accept his anger as normal, and now we laugh about his projecting so much power onto me.

"Ted, the youngest, felt cheated because the older boys had lived with their father longer than he had. After six months of complaining, he took the risk and asked to live with his father. I conceded, with the provision that Greg have the same choice. Greg decided to stay home, wanting to be with his friends instead of moving to his father's city apartment. I suddenly became a parent of one teenager rather than three, which required further adjustments.

"We lived through the trauma, apparently unscarred. I strove to maintain day-to-day routines, keeping the boys' needs for fathering and mothering in mind. I developed more outside interests in order to avoid becoming dependent on Greg for company. I enjoy my work, friends, and scattered family."

Other single mothers have found solutions to their problems by joining families who are also dealing with single parenthood.

"I had been a single parent for several years and had little difficulty with my two children. I began floundering when they began adolescence, my son at thirteen and my daughter at eleven. I felt rejected when they began moving away from me emotionally, and realized I was quite dependent on their companionship. I received another blow when my ex-husband stopped sending money for the children's support, just when expenses were increasing. A friend of mine suggested we join households and share parenting. He had custody of his three teenagers and was more experienced than I about handling adolescents. The children were friends and quickly agreed to the move.

"We've lived together for two years, and it's working. Friends soon accepted our unconventional family, and we're too busy to care about gossipers. We are not lovers. Our rented house is large enough for each family's privacy. We share expenses, eat communally, everyone pitches in with housework, and we adults don't feel so alone with our parenting responsibilities. I had assumed my son would latch onto Larry as a surrogate father since his own dad rarely visits him. He likes Larry as a friend, and has other substitute fathers, like his football coach and athletic heroes.

"Larry and I have a rule to pursue our love interests away from home, taking turns being in charge when either goes away for the weekend. Other divorced friends of mine have merged their families; some with other women and one with an older couple. We all feel that having other adults in the home relieves the burdens of single parenthood."

Therese shares her problem by explaining, "My struggles are complex and unresolvable. I know my fourteen-year-old daughter will eventually grow up, but at present our strife seems endless. I divorced Ellen's father when she was twelve. She is unforgiving and berates me for taking away her idealized father. She begs to live with him. Ethically, I can't allow her to grow up with an alcoholic. He has no desire to raise Ellen, but charms her with promises of 'some day we'll get you away from your mother.'

"When he remembers, he takes her to expensive restaurants, lavishing gifts, and treats on her in a kingly fashion. She readily forgives his missed appointments because he's so persuasive and enchanting when he calls. I am the ogre. She verbalizes her anger and dislike for me daily, and we live in an unhappy atmosphere. I would revel in exposing her father's lies and drinking problem, but it would only add to her misery and sense of being a victim. I maintain sanity in group therapy sessions for single parents. Sharing frustrations helps, and gives me hope that one day Ellen will appreciate my position."

A single parent's feeling of isolation can be further increased by worries about money. Single parents with custody rights very often have financial difficulties, as child-support payments frequently fail to cover expenses or may not arrive at all.

Single parents usually resent the seemingly carefree life of their divorced spouses, whose lives appear glamorous, being removed from teenager's daily complaints, bickering, illnesses, and need for affection, reassurance, and attention.

Many single parents, although they appreciate the personal freedom when children visit "the other one," feel that part-time, weekend, holiday, or summer parents spoil the children. Life with the everyday parent involves rules, planning, sacrifice, and routine. Visiting time with the absent parent is associated with treats, presents, trips, and freedom from restrictive authority. Every time children return from visits, they remourn the bond loss, resent the return to normal living conditions, and reexperience anger at the home parent. They must readjust to daily life once more. These separations from the visited parent are stressful to children and single parents alike, who are made to feel like bad guys in face of the returning children's anger.

In order to recover the balance and harmony between the home parent and returning teenagers, an open flow of talk must be encouraged. The adult must try to understand objectively that the children's anger and sorrow are normal. Equilibrium is quickly reestablished when children are encouraged to express their feelings. Adolescents should not be made to feel disloyal when they maintain intense love feelings for the absent parent. Parental love is precious to them and should not be manipulated by either parent. Parents who demand love and loyalty, and maneuver children into hating the absent parent pay a dear price with discerning teenagers. Of course it's tempting to expose the ex-spouse as an evil person, but teenagers do not want to listen to negative stories about either parent, nor do they enjoy being used as go-betweens, being asked to send or bring messages designed to infuriate ex-mates.

One mother with two teenage girls and a pre-teen son found that talking about their feelings wasn't enough. "We all decided that the best thing for all of us would be to have a good scream. We counted to three and all let out the biggest bellows we could manage. We screamed ourselves out after ten minutes. The release was wonderful."

Some single parents find themselves devoting too much time and attention to their offspring. They suddenly discover that they are living *for* their children instead of *with* them. The habit is easy to form, as children are safer to deal with than potentially hurtful adults. This situation can cause future problems if the parent remarries. The children, used to being the center of attention, resent having to share a parent once again.

The Divorced Father

In recent years growing numbers of men have become the custodial parent either by mutual consent or by court decree.

"Our problems are similar to women who parent alone," comments George, the father of two teenagers. "My marriage ended two years ago. My ex-wife decided to return to college and announced I would be taking care of our daughters. I gladly accepted. The girls, then thirteen and fifteen, were delighted to have me all to themselves. The practical management of the apartment went smoothly. Without my conscious awareness, the girls began to act like miniature wives, competing for my attention. After the rejection I felt when my wife divorced me, I basked in their attention and affection.

"My sister visited and pronounced me a 'regressive father' who was holding the girls back from normal pursuits. 'You've encouraged a family romance by letting the kids act like a couple of wives. You must find women your own age instead of enjoying all this adoration. Are you afraid to risk adult love again?' Her blunt interpretation made me recognize that I was taking advantage of my daughters' attachment. I had to undo my mistakes. They acted hurt when I resumed dating. I brought a woman home for dinner, and they were rude and disruptive. Fortunately, my date had a teenage son who had become possessive after her divorce. She said parents must take responsibility when teenagers act like mates instead of kids. She said, 'Tell them you were hurt and needy and using them for solace and talk about getting back to parent-child delineations. You'll all be happier.'

"I broached the delicate subject with my girls and we all discovered some interesting emotional undercurrents in our behavior. They admitted that a great deal of their wifely play-acting was to prove their superiority to their mother. They were angry about her desertion and hoped she would visit and feel guilty and inferior when she witnessed our cozy trio. I confessed to using them for healing my wounds. We were denying our resentments about the mother and wife who blithely left us to follow her own interests. Our talks about hidden motivations and feelings connected with divorce stimulated my daughters to begin a 'Teenage Seminar on Children of Divorce.' They talk with schoolmates about normal responses when one parent leaves. Their group became so popular that they were invited on a local television show to explain their group.

"I joined Parents Without Partners to further understand and cope with our family life."

Parents Without Partners is for parents who are divorced, separated, widowed, or who were never married. It is an educational organization devoted to the welfare and interest of single parents and their offspring. With professional help, programs are conducted in which lectures, discussions, publications, and recreational activities aid the single parent in coping with problems. In discussion groups people talk out their problems and share experiences, sympathetically and with understanding, helping single parents gain a new perspective as they discover that they are not alone and that others have triumphed over similar difficulties. Recreational and social activities, for both adults and children, provide a comfortable environment for interaction free of the fifth-wheel feeling.

The Visiting Parent

The visiting parent, usually the father, has many conflicting emotions to handle. After divorce he loses a section of his identity—as husband and everyday parent. This identity shock leaves scars of failure and family loneliness. Parents who see their teenagers rarely always speak wistfully of how they daily miss their rapidly changing teenagers' voices, their school activities, their friends' visits, casual affection, and all the back-and-forth daily contact with one's own.

During parental visits, the time together is so brief that the reasonable visitation rights always seem unfairly regulated. The permeating sense of unreality when teenagers are to be entertained like company also cloud the relationship. The visited or visiting parent often behaves like Santa Claus, because of guilt and a fear of confrontation about unresolved feelings. Adolescents will gladly play the game of demanding more presents and treats if they sense a parent's uneasiness and guilt.

Lurking underneath the holiday atmosphere are insecure teenagers and a nervous adult. Teenagers are afraid to talk about their anger caused by the divorce, by changes in their life-style, and by their ultimate abandonment by one parent. They sense their anger will further alienate the lost parent. The parent fears loss of love will occur if these sticky issues are addressed head on. Emotionally speaking, the opposite is true. Encouraging free-flowing discussions, questions, and expressions of disappointment, grief, and anger clear the air, allowing family members to relax and be themselves.

Depending on the maturity of the adolescent, queries should be answered directly and truthfully. Self-confident parents have the opportunity to explain their position and reaffirm that parental love is not disrupted because of divorce between adults. Visiting or visited teenagers need reassurance, love, and honesty. These gifts will be treasured and remembered long after expensive gifts are outgrown.

Parents without custody can maintain family feelings with teenagers by keeping in touch as much as possible. Letters and phone calls between visits keep the promise of care alive. Time together can be natural and casually loving if everyone talks about their feelings. Being natural includes observing rules for appropriate behavior and discipline and avoiding the image of the all-perfect wonderful, gift-giving, part-time mom or dad.

The Deserted Family

The single parent who must cope alone because of desertion has the most difficult of child-rearing tasks. Teenagers find it difficult to incorporate the fact that a parent would leave them, never to return. Denying the reality, many deserted adolescents conjure exaggerated, idealized fantasies about the lost parents, "parenting" themselves through daydreams. They imagine the parent returning and rescuing them from the hardships of adolescence.

The remaining parent can do nothing but endure these fantasies until teenagers develop the emotional maturity to handle the reality of desertion. The daydreams are a necessary defense against rejection feelings which are too painful to deal with.

Choosing Single Parenthood

Women who choose childbirth and motherhood without marriage make the decision from the position of self-determination. They do not have to deal with the traumas of separation and divorce, as they expected to parent alone when they chose conception.

The problem of choosing to be the only parent hits women when they realize the extent to which the child depends solely on them for emotional, physical, and financial support.

Mary chose to become pregnant without the man's knowledge. She chose a stranger who was healthy and attractive. "I was down on all men and had the fantasy that my child would grow up as a perfect person without having to be influenced by some neurotic father. I had a vision of my baby and me facing life together in a cloud of untroubled love. The reality was quite different than the dream. I worked at home as a free-lance writer and thought everything would be simple, not knowing how much care babies need.

"Having a boy was the first shock, as I had assumed I would deliver a girl—the two of us showing the world how wonderful a mother and daughter can be together, without a man. Life worked itself along, and I didn't miss having a husband. However, when Joey was two, and with increasing fervor, he asked every man in sight, 'Are you my Daddy?' I didn't need or want a man, but my son did. He's thirteen now and resents the fact that he doesn't have or know his father. I feel guilty because I never took into consideration the feelings of the unborn person."

The Death of a Parent

Single parenting because of death presents unique problems.

Teenagers may withdraw into a private world of mourning, unable to cry or express remorse. Others assume quasi-maturity and deny feelings by taking charge and comforting others behind a mask of strength.

Anger is expected when divorce disrupts a teenager's life. Adults assume teenagers are sorrowful and bereft when a parent dies, and they encourage expressions of grief. These emotions are present, but often feel insincere unless the survivor's normal anger is confronted.

Teenagers who still invest superhuman powers in adults often think a parent has deliberately rejected them by choosing death. They feel cheated of the normal progression of debonding when death severs the relationship. They may harbor anger toward the remaining parent, sure there was some way the adult could have warded off death. Frequently, adolescents feel angry at themselves, assuming their behavior or thoughts magically caused the parent's death.

"My wife died in a car crash. Jeremy, thirteen, was stoic during the funeral and silently withdrew in the following weeks. I was dazed, an emotional wreck with nothing to offer my children. My mother stayed on after the funeral, comforting me and the two younger girls. She could not reach or even physically touch Jeremy. In desperation when he refused to eat, she took Jeremy to our doctor. She sat in the waiting room for an hour, wondering why the examination was so lengthy. A crying Jeremy burst from the inner office and flung himself on her, sobbing, 'I didn't really kill Mom.'

"Later, the doctor related that many teenagers suffer crushing guilt when a parent dies. 'They have normal hostile feelings for parents and often wish the controlling parent would disappear. Since parents rarely die, they can be comfortable with their fantasies. Your son was at the mother-distancing stage and was irritated by her protective nature. He was convinced he had caused her accident because of his secret wishes. He thought his own death would pay for his crime and was planning on starving to death. I told him he wasn't a killer, but a normal boy whose mother would want him to grow up and be happy.'"

Whichever form anger takes—self-loathing, blaming adults, feeling victimized by fate, depression, withdrawal—the single parent's job is to help the teenager face survivor's anger and accept the feelings as an integral part of mourning.

"When I was sixteen, my father died," remembers Evan. "I couldn't bear the emptiness inside of me. For a year, I kept him alive by taking on his mannerisms in an exaggerated form. I tried to be a protective man with my mother and sister, and lost my own personality. Even though my mom kept telling me to be myself, I couldn't give up my dad's personality traits.

"A friend's father died of cancer and I went to his house to offer condolences, patting him on the shoulder like my father would have done. He punched me and started screaming and crying like a wild man. Something broke inside of my carefully constructed shell and I began to cry about my dad for the first time. We blubbered together and I began the process of genuine mourning.

"Working out grief means crying for your loss, anger at a parent for dying, and spending time on memories to emotionally bury the dead. You eventually accept the death as final. I still feel longing for dad, but at least I'm over the hardest part. I wish my mother or some adult had known enough to get me crying right after he died so I would have avoided pretending to be him for that long, long year."

Early Maturity

Children of single parents, as they develop and understand the circumstances and limitations of their parents, mature faster and create coping devices to deal with their reality. They also learn that happiness can be enjoyed even if they do not have two parents in the home.

NINE

Stepparents and Teenagers

Raising someone else's children is the most unappreciated part of parenting. Stepchildren are definitely not grateful for a stepparent's services, since they usually experience a stepparent as an interloper in their family. As we discussed earlier, most children carry the fantasy that their divorced parents will reunite someday. A stepparent in the family throws cold water on that fantasy. The natural parent does not receive the particular variety of hostility that is directed toward the stepparent and finds it difficult to understand the stepparent's complaints. The absent parent most likely resents the stepparent, as the stepparent is his or her replacement and seems superior both as husband or wife and parent. A stepparent is supposed to love the offspring who emerged from one much-loved adult and one hated adult, the ex-mate of one's beloved. From every angle, stepparenting is a difficult job that requires tact, humor, a thick skin, and self-confidence.

The Absent Bond

Many stepparents feel guilty because they do not develop strong love feelings for their stepchildren. This guilt is needless because stepparents and their instant families do not have the psychological

153

bonds which naturally occur with biological parents and their children. Stepchildren do not have the woven fabric of emotional connections with their stepparents. When this bond is absent, there are no automatic tugs to the heart, feelings of protection, or concerns which natural parents take for granted. Stepparents who accept the fact of lesser feelings as normal can expend energies developing a friendship with stepchildren, instead of worrying about their lack of strong feelings for them.

As teenagers are distancing from the bonds with parents, they have little problem disconnecting from stepparents, since no deep bond is present. Naive stepparents who try to construct bonds with teenagers are usually met with indifference. Teenagers don't want closeness with any authority figures, least of all parents. Understanding the nature of debonding can assist stepparents who feel rejected when they try to get close to bristly adolescents.

Accepting the Stepparent into the Family

When you enter an already formed family, expect outright or subtle rejection from your stepchildren. Preparing for snubs arms you to deal with the frustrations and surprises when stepchildren pretend that you don't exist.

Children whose parents remarry have been through many emotional trials. They have witnessed the disintegration of the parents' love, experienced the bond loss of one parent, changed life-styles, and made adjustments to living with a single parent. They have become used to paying attention to one parent, and it is natural for them to turn to their natural parent for advice, money, and conversation. It takes time for them to assimilate another adult into the family. Children who have lived in a single-parent family are used to receiving more adult attention than is possible when both husband and wife are there, living and loving together. They must adjust to sharing their parent's attention with a stepparent, and in the beginning they often resent this sharing.

All families have their established routines, which the new parent must now fit into. This adjustment requires the ability to accommodate oneself to other people's habits and need of privacy.

Just because two adults love each other does not mean that their children will be pleased for them or like their choices. Normally self-involved teenagers have no sympathy for parental need of love and romance. If you don't expect their sympathy, you won't be disappointed.

A woman who married a man with a ten-year-old daughter and two teenage sons recounted her wedding. "I was thrilled to marry Tom and had spent some time with his children. He had been their only parent since their mother died several years before. I had visions and plans about becoming their replacement mother. The boys didn't even want to come to the wedding because there was a motocross race that day. They were forced into respectable clothes and stood around looking mean and angry during the ceremony and reception. Jill, Tom's daughter, was cute and acted like a hostess.

"Daily living was a complete shock to me. Jill resented my attempts at mothering, as she was a competent little person who liked to cook her own breakfast and didn't want me fussing over her. The boys tended to ignore me and were unimpressed with my gourmet cooking. They didn't want souffles and special sauces, just good old hamburgers and hot dogs. Jill politely interrupted my conversations with her dad, and kept reminding me that I put all the utensils in the wrong drawer.

"They treated me like a nuisance as I fussed and clamored for their approval. My husband finally said, 'Why don't you just relax and be yourself and let the kids come to you?' His solution was so simple that I had overlooked it. I was treating the children like poor orphans when actually they were all pretty well adjusted and didn't need my meddling. We're all friends now, and they tease me about my 'fairy godmother' routine when I first joined the family."

She talked further about the need for stepparents to think of themselves as joining an existing family instead of creating a new one. She also discussed the fact that people who try to be the perfect new parents almost always fail in their own eyes and bug the stepchildren with their need for instant approval.

Our personal and clinical experience has shown that stepparent acceptance usually takes a year or two. If stepparents are comfortable within themselves, don't push for quick rapport, and respect teenagers' need to be distant, then the adjustments come quicker.

Teenagers respond well to light banter because it doesn't involve criticism or control. Such easy going talk gives stepparents an arena of conflict-free space in which to relate to young people.

Problems of Discipline

Stepchildren do not take kindly to a "stranger" telling them what to do. Besides, they resent commands and orders from all adults during their years of becoming independent. The new couple will find life easier if they discuss long-standing family rules and expected modes of behavior and discipline in order to avoid foolish blunders by the stepparent.

We have found it unworkable to have just the natural parent set and administer guidelines for behavior. In that case, the children tend to see the stepparent as just another child who is powerless. It's frustrating for an adult to be told, "You can't tell me what to do; you're not my real mom (dad)." This notion is absurd, as all children receive instructions from other adults all the time. If a stepmother is home all day, she must make countless decisions for and with the children. "Wait until your father gets home" can be very ineffective if a hulking teenager decides to sit on a younger sibling.

Teenagers respond to requests more than to commands. The polite approach allows them their dignity as they are cheerfully asked to perform a job rather than being told to do something. Most teenagers have a built-in "molasses factor" when any adult tells them to do anything. Normally quick, coordinated teenagers seem struck by slowness when a parent asks a question or gives an order. This "moving through molasses" response is a sign of their assertion of independence. Teenagers want to carry out requests in their own time in order to feel that they have some control. Stepparents do not have to take this response as a defiant gesture against them, but can accept it as normal teenage behavior.

Comparisons with the Natural Parent

A stepparent should also expect to receive negative comparisons in the beginning of the new marriage. As the absent parent is often idealized, there is no way the stepparent can come out on top, even if he or she is kinder, more loving, and more generous than the natural parent, for the child must maintain the fantasy of the perfect, lost parent.

The major area for comparison of stepmothers with natural mothers is in the area of food. Since a mother is the original giver of food from infancy on, food is equated with her love. A stepmother's food cannot replace the unconscious feelings of love connected to the original mother. Even if a stepmother follows the recipe of her stepchildren's mother, the outcome will never be "just right." Do not try to rival or compete with the cooking of your mate's ex-wife. Find out what the children like to eat, do your best, and let the comments bounce off.

A client of ours married a man with two teenage girls. When she saw them eating cold cereal for breakfast, she decided to show them what a special treat breakfast could be. The next morning she had freshly squeezed orange juice, little toast cups filled with scrambled eggs and diced ham, fried tomatoes topped with cheddar cheese, and steaming mugs of hot chocolate. "The girls looked at my presentation with dismay, pushed the food around on their plates for a while, and abruptly left for school. They called their dad at his office during the day wanting to know what to do about me.

"Meanwhile I was crushed and disappointed after all the work I had done and the changes I had planned for their better nutrition. Thankfully, my husband told the girls to settle their own problems with me, instead of putting him in the position of a go-between. The girls came home from school and offered me a candy bar—the kind of gloppy mess that only teenagers love. When I declined, they said, 'Well, that's how we feel about breakfast. We don't like eggs and stuff in the morning, just cereal.'" She learned the lesson of not barging in, projecting her notions onto the girls. "I now save my breakfast productions for my husband and my Sunday brunch, and the girls still enjoy their cereal, relieved that I leave them alone."

Many stepparents who are marrying for the first time have an expectation that the family will sit down together at the table and enjoy leisurely meals and conversation, just as in a Norman Rockwell painting. Teenagers, however, often do not want this family scene and prefer to eat on the run or sometimes take a plate to their room. If this practice has become a routine in the family, stepparents will find more acceptance if they do not interfere.

If stepchildren complain and criticize your food, agree with them and suggest they make a sandwich for themselves. If you handle the negative comparisons with mom's cooking lightly, food will cease to be an issue.

Stepfathers receive the major comparison in the area of physical power. The biological father is always seen as stronger, more competent, and more aggressive than his replacement. This view is not an attack on the stepfather but a need to sustain the natural father in the position of kindly strength.

If all comparisons are handled with humor, the teenage stepchild soon gives up the need to devalue the stepparent. It's no fun to tear down a person who can laugh at his or her own shortcomings.

Jealousy on Two Fronts

Stepparents should assume that jealousy will be present in their new family mix. Children will feel jealous as "the intruder" takes first place with the parent who was giving them exclusive attention. Even though teenagers are distancing themselves from parents, they still feel jealous when the parent falls in love and brings a new person into the home.

If stepchildren visit, they will resent having to share attention with the parent's new spouse. If visits are infrequent, wise stepparents make sure that the children and their parent spend time alone together.

"Just after we were married, my two stepdaughters came for the summer," remembers Doris. "They resented me immediately. I thought the three of us would have a lot in common as I was twenty-five and they were thirteen and fifteen. I was in for a few surprises.

"Their father was gone all day and they sat around with glum faces, watching television and looking through me when I suggested doing anything together. I felt totally rejected and ill-equipped to deal with this kind of ugliness. Nightly, when my husband returned, the sullen twosome changed into charming ingenues. I had chilling thoughts of throttling them which jostled my view of myself as a non-violent person. I refused to compete for their father's attention and kind of slunk around in the background and kept quiet when we all went out.

"Naturally, he loved their adoration and their cheerful dispositions. I thought it would be childish to recount to him how badly they treated me, and, frankly, didn't want to admit my inability to deal with two kids. Three months is a long time to put up with constant rejections. I sorted through my feelings and discovered I was afraid of them and avoiding any kind of hostile encounter.

"I convinced myself that nothing they could say could be worse than being ignored and feeling like an outcast in my own home. I was hesitant to request their help with the increased housework for fear they would complain to their father and he would resent my treatment of his darling girls. I was responding to the stress like a helpless child, and decided I had to take control over my senseless fears.

"The next morning they flopped in front of the television set to space out until the evening. I turned the set off and I'll relate our unfriendly confrontation.

"Your wicked stepmother has to talk to her innocent stepchildren, or I'm going to toss you both out the door and lock it until your dad comes home?"

"Huh!"

"Oh, God!"

"It's either that or some straight talking. We're wasting energies in this silent war between us."

"Well, we didn't start it!"

"Did I?"

"You don't want us to visit our dad! You want him all to yourself."

"I'd like to enjoy your visit, but you both treat me like a disease."

"Mom said you broke up her marriage. She says Dad will divorce you and come back to us."

"Let's straighten that one out. Did you know I met your father a year after his divorce? How could I have been the culprit in your parents' divorce?"

"I dunno."

"She said he was having an affair with a younger woman."

"It wasn't me. I may be younger than your mother, but you two make me feel like an ancient witch."

"Really. Too bad for you."

"So, why do you hate me? Let's be as gross as possible."

"Well, you act jealous when Dad pays attention to us."

"I feel jealous because you're both so nice to him and so mean to me."

"We're not mean!"

"Mean is not giving a person a chance to be friends. Mean is glowering at me when I suggest things. Mean is pretending I don't exist. And, I guess I've been mean by not thinking about your feelings."

"I hate coming from a broken home."

"I would too. The reality is that your folks did divorce, and even if I wasn't your dad's new wife your parents wouldn't remarry. I agree that must be hard to accept. If you do, maybe we can stop being mean and start being a little kind."

"We want to spend time with just Dad, and you always come along."

"I'll stay home some nights and you three can go to the show or out to eat."

"Super!"

"How about if I just left home for the summer. You gals could take care of the house, cook your dad's meals, do the laundry, pay the bills, and do all those fun errands for him? I could go on my own vacation."

"Huh?"

"You could have him all to yourselves."

"You can stay and keep house, Doris, that's okay."

"Did you know that's the first time either of you has called me Doris. You usually refer to me as 'she' or 'her.' I suddenly feel like a person. Let's all say anything we feel from now on and maybe we can learn to get along."

"Will you still let us go out with Dad alone?"

"Sure, just keep calling me Doris."

The confrontation broke the ice and softened hostilities on both sides.

"This summer the girls visited again and we bantered about our cold war of the previous year. They can't relate to me as a second mother, but at least we've started to be friends. I make sure they get exclusive time with their father, and my increased feelings of security as a loved wife have erased my left out feelings.

"Several of my friends married older men with teenagers and they all experienced varying degrees of rejection, mainly from daughters. I've advised them to start talking honestly instead of hoping negative feelings will be resolved with placation or silent suffering."

Adults are often surprised when they feel jealous of children. But stepparents are not invincible in the face of the green-eyed monster. Parents and their offspring have a bond that has been growing many years before the stepparent entered the picture. It does no good to seethe jealously about a spouse's love for the children, since paternal and maternal love are totally different from heterosexual love.

Talking about jealousy is a good cure for both stepchildren and stepparents. Teenagers are amazed that anyone could be envious of them, as they spend considerable time worrying about their inadequacies. An honest talk, on equal footing, can reassure everyone that there is love enough for everyone.

Stepparents must try to overcome jealous feelings if spouses and ex-mates remain friends. It's good for the children to see that, although their parents couldn't stay married, at least they are mature enough to maintain friendly relations. When stepparents accept the fact that they are not a part of the past (good and bad), feelings of exclusion are eased.

Ambivalent Feelings

Experiencing two opposing feelings for a person is distinctly confusing. Teenagers have a variety of vacillating reactions about themselves, friends, teachers, and parents, which they try to sort out. When the stepparent enters the picture, they must deal with the feelings of "intruder" jealousy, resentment, and adjustment to a new person. They may grow to like the new adult as it becomes evident that the stepparent brings happiness to the natural parent. They may even learn to love a stepparent who respects their privacy, relates to them as young adults, and doesn't interfere with their freedom.

Ambivalence arises when teenagers feel guilty about loving or liking a stepparent. A feeling of being disloyal to the real parent causes the guilt, which is a vestige of childhood thinking that loving one person takes away from good feelings for another. Parents can discuss these feelings by explaining that love expands when shared with many people.

The stepparent may be troubled about feeling both love and hate for stepchildren. Such ambivalence is normal in all close relationships—ask any "real" parent.

Resentments about Money

Money management, so rarely discussed during courtship, can cause marital strife in connection with stepchildren. Since in many marriages both husband and wife work, stepparents often feel resentful paying expenses for their inherited children. The stepchild may not accept the new parent—while at the same time enjoying the food, clothing, and luxuries that the stepparent helps provide. Stepparents also feel used as their mates continue to pay child-support at the expense of vacations or recreation. Hidden beneath these indignations are unrealistic expectations of gratitude. By nature teenagers do not appreciate adult sacrifices, either of time or of money. They are even less grateful to a stepparent who disrupted their lives by marrying their single parent.

Older Stepchildren

Often a man will marry a young woman to whom his older teenage children cannot relate as a mother figure, a situation that usually develops after the late-adolescent children are away at college. In such cases, young stepmothers should try to be friends with their semi-adult stepchildren.

An attractive young woman dealt sensibly with a sticky issue. At her wedding, she met, for the first time, her stepson, a younger replica of his handsome father. An immediate sexual attraction caused distress to the bride and mischievous seductivity in the young man. "I was surprised at myself at first, and then realized I would be physically attracted to this beautiful creature no matter what the circumstances. I decided to dress conservatively when he came to visit and made sure we were not put in tempting situations. He is a great teaser, just like my husband, so we manage to laugh about our original attraction. My husband isn't jealous, and he thinks it's normal for everyone to be attracted to me."

Without the family barrier against incest, sexual encounters can occur between stepparents and their mate's offspring. Mature recognition of the fact, and sublimation of the feelings into friendship, can alleviate feelings of discomfort for the adult.

Teenagers may be unaware of a sexual attraction toward a

stepparent and act out feelings with irritating conduct, moodiness, or blatant animosity—sometimes a defense against distress-producing sexual feelings.

"My wife's seventeen-year-old daughter was quite seductive with me when I was dating her mother," explained Tom, a handsome man in his forties. "I ignored her sexy glances by acting unperceiving. I naively assumed that after our marriage Liz would see me as a father figure and drop her sexy games. I have no children of my own and thought that teenagers were rational mini-adults.

"One afternoon when my wife was at the beauty parlor Liz startled me in the living room by appearing in shorty pajamas and said, 'Let's get it on.' I was embarrassed, angry, and discombobulated. I blurted that I was her stepfather, not a potential lover. 'Why don't you get dressed and we'll talk about some family rules,' I muttered, leaving the room for safer quarters. She flounced out, slammed her bedroom door, and refused to come out when her mother returned home.

"I didn't share the incident with my wife and mentioned that Liz and I were having an adjustment problem. I didn't feel as confident as I sounded. Liz ignored me for days and then became sarcastic. Her contempt was much easier for me to handle than the physical advances had been. I spoke with her privately, saying, 'I don't really believe you want to be seductive or hateful. I don't think you know what you want from me. Let's back up and try to understand your real feelings.' She burst into tears.

"I held her hands while she wept like a little, lost orphan. In between sobs she admitted feeling jealous and shoved aside by me and wanted to prove I was a bastard by seducing me. These feelings were present even though she had her own circle of good friends and dates. After she calmed down, I convinced her that jealousy and anger were normal reactions when parents remarry. I told her she could trust me to listen to her feelings which would be more helpful than playing games which ended up hurting her, causing more isolation. She's twenty now and has left home. Recently, she apologized for her crazy antics when she was a 'mixed-up kid.'

"Hindsight reveals to me that I should have taken action when she first began flirting before our family began. However, I was inexperienced with teenagers and their peculiar ways of dealing with feelings."

A stepmother recalled that her fifteen-year-old stepson was sexually attracted to her. "I was very uncomfortable around Sandy because he kept staring at my body. When I glanced his way, he would quickly look away, blush and soon afterward, behave grossly by passing gas, belching, or swearing at the dog, forcing his father to reprimand him.

"I had no desire to be the object of his sexual interests. There seemed no way to discuss this unspoken problem without upsetting him. He would probably have denied his feelings and the tensions would surely have increased. In order to remove myself as a sexual figure I began directing conversations to Sandy's studies and athletic interests, and always ended up talking about girls in his class. Gradually, by my presenting myself as an older female advisor, his attraction lessened and was successfully repressed. I never appeared in scanty clothing or entered his room without first knocking. My casual, helpful approach eased his attraction away from my figure. What a relief!"

Solutions to Stress

A couple we know who blended five children from previous marriages have a release system that helps them maintain their sanity. "We set aside time for being defensive about 'my wonderful children' and let each other blow off steam about all the kids' manipulations, inconsiderations, and rudeness—anything that bugs us. We have children whose ages range from six to twenty, so you can imagine the complaints we have. It's interesting how impatient you can get with other people's children and how easy it is to dismiss your own kid's irritating mannerisms and habits.

"We felt so much better after our ranting sessions that we figured the children would enjoy the same opportunity to freely rave on about their injustices. We give anyone who feels like griping our undivided attention. They know they can say anything they want without fear of censure, and it helps them voice their angers and complaints. It was hardest on my husband's children, because my family moved into his house, forcing his brood to share their space."

This tool relieves even the minor annoyances that are inevitable when two families attempt to become one.

Another couple tried to ease family tensions by arranging one weekend a month without children. They try to give themselves some privacy in order to strengthen their marriage bond and get to know each other, without the distraction of children banging around.

Since remarried people and stepparents must deal with many more stresses and strains than carefree newlyweds, friendship in marriage is of prime importance. Couples should feel that they can honestly discuss issues about children as well as negative feelings, disappointments, and anger under the safety of a continually growing friendship. When children witness the deep bonds of loving friendship between a parent and stepparent, they feel more secure and less threatened by the newcomer.

If you are a stepparent of a teenager, keep these reminders in mind as you guide your family through these developmental years:

> Have realistic expectations. The new family will require time and patience (mostly on the parent's part) to adjust to you.
>
> Expect criticism and learn to handle it with humor. Don't worry if you can't learn to love stepchildren with whom you have no natural bond.
>
> Learn about teenagers in order to accept normal rebellion as their own trip—not as a personal attack.
>
> Be flexible as you fit into established routines.
>
> Let stepchildren idealize lost parents; they would do it whether or not you were around.
>
> Don't expect gratitude for rearing someone else's offspring.
>
> Talk about all feelings with your mate, or with people in similar circumstances if your spouse cannot understand your problems. Remember that you are an adult, and can sort out feelings and reactions more reasonably than a teenager.
>
> Try to become a friend to your stepchildren instead of trying to replace the special spot that is reserved for the natural parent. Remember that children really do leave home someday.

TEN

Late-Adolescence

Late-adolescence heralds freedom for teenagers. These years before settling down to adult pursuits offer opportunities to explore possibilities for the future, enrich and broaden perspectives by travel or further education, experiment with relationships, and solidify personality characteristics. Young adults define themselves and are judged as separate people, rather than as someone's son or daughter.

Many mistakes will be made by late-teenagers when they test their skills and growing self-sufficiency in the expanding world of college, work, and relationships. Their youthful vitality makes it possible for them to recover from errors, survive and attempt further challenges.

The teenager's struggle for independence and the process of debonding should be completed during the high school years in order to devote energies to dealing with personal freedom. The parents' role is less demanding as children leave home for college, travel, or to live with friends. It is a time to encourage young people to take pride in their resourcefulness while still offering emotional support and guidance when asked. Parents normally see little of their late adolescent children. Even if young people remain at home, their interests are directed toward friends and love relationships.

Time Out for Travel and Adventure

Many adventurous adolescents thrill to new possibilities, packing up their belongings as they decide to explore the country to take a breather from plans, schedules, and decisions for a year or more. They want to experience other life-styles, meet large varieties of new people, and learn how to get by. The grapevine of information among road travelers tells wandering youths where to spend the night, whom to look up in certain cities, and what possible hassles to avoid.

Adults are often amazed at the casual attitude of young people as they welcome half-strangers into their homes after only vague acquaintance. They leave their belongings in the care of strangers, sure that when they pass through again, the goods will still be there. Wandering youths find out quickly whom to trust, learn much from experiences with rip-off artists, and become proficient at working odd jobs. The majority of adventurers we have known have a wonderful time.

Parents reared in the "education-equals-success" era often fear that these adventurers will lose out if they do not move smoothly from high school into college. Concerned parents also have realistic worries about physical harm befalling their trusting adventurers. Parental worry about disrupting a hoped-for career is unfounded. Many people who have taken off a year after high school graduation have discovered that they have had more maturity to handle college when they returned. Some find interesting work, which they would never have been exposed to if they remained at home or went off to college. If the need for freedom is not satisfied by exploring, the young person can become a bored and uninterested college student. Parental trepidation about physical injury is very real, but we cannot lock young people into their rooms until life proves itself safe. The wandering backpacker quickly develops safety and survival techniques, and learns how to judge strangers' motivations and how to cope with the environment.

The question that faces many parents is whether they should finance their late-teenager's year or so of travel and adventure. As beneficial as this exploration of the world is for many people, it is more maturing for them when they take their own financial responsibility. All growth and expanding experiences have more meaning and value if people provide for themselves. If a young person seeks to declare independence from the family, yet allows parents to finance the wanderlust, the potential young adult turns out to be just a vacationing dependent. Parents who wish to finance a traveler may think that through their financing they have some control over their children's activities, but this is rarely the case. True autonomy means taking care of oneself, including making the money to enjoy the freedom of the road.

"Our son saved his money during high school, preparing for European travel," recalls Louise about her adventurous son, "and explored different cultures for two years. He was a gregarious and resourceful person, so we knew he would benefit from meeting new people and learning to adjust to different countries' social climates. Thankfully, he kept in touch with occasional letters, alleviating our concerns about his health and whereabouts. He worked at various jobs when his money ran out, had several romantic interludes, and made many new friends. After his return he told us of being robbed at knifepoint once, being lost several times, and almost drowning in a boat accident. We were relieved he waited until his return to share those adventures.

"His years of travel matured him, adding to his self-assurance, knowledge, and turned him into an entertaining story-teller. During his journey he had decided to become a writer. He kept notebooks, jotting down quick descriptions and impressions of people for use in future novels. He decided to take advantage of a trust fund set up for his education and entered college to hone his writing skills.

"We rarely see him because he travels around the country during the summer. When he does visit, we enjoy his company, even though the time is always brief.

"We encourage our friends to give their blessings to children who express a desire for travel. If they are intent on exploring, they will find a way to follow their dreams even if parents disapprove."

"I have four daughters," relates a father, "and, after high school, they all left home for life on the road. They flew from New York to California and worked their way back across the country. I worried the most about my first traveler, fearful of rape, muggers, and dope dealers. However, I soon realized that these hazards were present in the city and she had excellent survival skills. By the time my last girl packed for her jaunt, I was resigned to my children's wanderlust. I've had several emergency collect calls over the years, mostly for a quick loan. I respond as long as repayment is promised and prompt. I don't expect to hear from them on a regular basis, because they're busy and involved with new life experiences.

"My youngest is still traveling and the others have become a doctor, an artist, and a psychologist. They are still single and live in New York.

"I wish I had been as carefree and venturesome when I was young. My children's roaming ways satisfied some basic need for adventure before they settled down. We're better friends today because I didn't interfere with their need to leave home."

The College Freshman

College freshmen also experience freedom from supervision and parents' rules, although in a more structured environment than the traveling late-teenager.

In order to make a successful adjustment to running one's own life, freshmen must learn to take personal responsibility for time, study, social, and money management—skills usually accomplished after a few months on campus. Those who prefer a sense of family join fraternities and sororities, which often results in life-long friendships.

College students rarely write letters to parents except for explanations of why they need more money. They like to receive mail from home, but only occasionally find time to reciprocate. They are busy and preoccupied, spending little time thinking about their parents' need to communicate with them. When visiting home, college students usually spend the majority of their time with friends, taking parents pretty much for granted. Parents may be eager to spend time with their maturing child and feel rebuffed when the visiting student fills his or her time with individual socializing. It is not a rejection but signifies further liberation from the family as the central focus for love and acceptance.

"I stayed home and attended a city university," relates a mother of a college student, "living in two worlds. At the university, I was on my own, but at home I still felt like a child in many ways, conforming to family rules and squabbling with my parents over my new ideas. I insisted that my son leave home for college. It's more maturing to live on campus, meeting and relating to different people, experimenting with new ideas, free from parental observation and opinions. It's very expensive, but he works part time and I gladly sacrifice for his opportunity to become a completely independent person. As a single parent I miss him and his friends around the apartment, but I raised him to leave home, not to be my companion."

College opens up doors to new worlds as young people meet and mingle with students from a variety of ethnic and social strata, with foreign students, and with people from other parts of the country. College can be a broadening experience as students open themselves up to exchanges between different viewpoints, decide on a vocation, and increase their capacities for intimacy in love and friendship. The pressure to be open and sincerely accepting of differences naturally leads students to experiment intellectually, socially, and sexually, outside the realm of parental control.

The World of Work

Graduating high-school seniors who move from school into the world of work must make the most considerable adjustments. In contrast to college freshmen, they enter a world no longer populated with peers but with a wide variety of adults whose ages span fifty or more years. The young person will no longer be treated as a student or be forgiven for teenage ways. Working means being responsible, performing consistently well, considering co-workers' rights, and accepting authority.

A friend of ours told of her shocking introduction to the reality of work when she took a day off after having worked as a secretary for three months. At 9:30 her boss called, asking why she wasn't at work.

"It's my birthday today."

"So what's that got to do with anything?" her irritated boss asked.

"I thought we all had the day off on our birthdays."

"Listen, kid, if you expect to have a job tomorrow, you better get your birthday ass into the office today," he bellowed before slamming down the phone.

She had learned the lesson that the outside world was not at all interested in her delight over her particular day of birth.

Late-adolescents who begin work deal with the loss of the friendship bonds and camaraderie of their high school days. New friends are hard to find in a new work environment because every person on the job has different personal interests: most are much older, some are married, some divorced; some are already parents; some are mean or sloppy, others happy and competent. Everyone seems involved in his or her own job, friends, and family. The new employee must somehow fit into the existing society.

If this is the young person's first introduction to the world of work, he or she will feel shy, insecure, and unsure of his or her abilities. Young employees who ask advice of older workers, who are willing to do extra work and try to be friendly and cooperative, earn acceptance from their co-workers. It can be a jolt to discover that no one is interested in the young person's life unless the new worker makes him- or herself likable. This unsentimental initiation into the cold, uncaring world feels like walking into a glass wall, one which offers no apology to the young adult who bumps into it.

Compared to all the positive and negative attention children have received during childhood, from both parents and teachers, the lack of interest on the part of the adults in the "real" world is a shock to still self-centered late-adolescents. This sobering experience pushes the young person further into maturity, as he realizes that career and social success depend upon one's ability to be assertive and unselfish. Resilient and optimistic young adults adjust to work realities, and self-esteem is enhanced as the working person feels like a significant adult, able to earn a living.

Most young people wish to set up apartments with friends or acquaintances. Finances are usually stretched, and young roommates are forced to sacrifice comforts by joining forces with three or more friends in order to afford living quarters away from home. Experiences with roommates and landlords teach young adults judgment and the art of adjusting to people outside the family circle.

Young people who work and remain at home should contribute to the finances of the house. Preparing for future and total independence requires paying one's way in the world. Teenagers should be told while they are still in high school that when they begin to work they will be expected to pay some money for room and board. When they are aware of future expectations, the shock of having to pay for what they took for granted will not be so great. Sharing expenses can become a symbol of the young person's new maturity.

Marriage

Some late-adolescents marry before they have completed the developmental tasks of this age group—emancipation from childhood ways, choice of a career, and solidification of a unique personality. Others master these tasks early and feel mature enough to handle the responsibilities of marriage.

Today's generation, brought up to make independent decisions, usually announces marriage plans to parents, rather than seeking approval or consent. Requesting late-adolescents to wait until they are more mature to commit themselves to marriage rarely meets with agreement. Couples in love feel omnipotent in the face of predictable marriage difficulties and divorce statistics. They approach marriage with great confidence, even if parents express concern and voice disapproval.

Young adults hope that parents will celebrate their decision. They may surprise everyone and find lasting satisfaction in their marriage. They may discover that marriage is stifling, their mate a disappointment, and seek divorce. Many early married and subsequently divorced people look back on their union and dissolution as another growth experience, some regretful and others nonchalant about the vicissitudes of love.

As with other decisions during late-adolescence, young people usually prefer to take their own chances, relying on personal judgment rather than considering parents' opinions deeply.

How parents relate to their late-adolescent children will determine their future mutual friendship. Parents can wisely follow a few simple guidelines while dealing with their almost-adult children:

Withhold advice, as you would with any other adult, unless specifically asked, changing gears from being the advisor to being an available experienced adult willing to share information.

Bestow appropriate praise. Praise from parents always carries special meaning for young adults.

Call your adult children adult names if the nicknames from childhood make them uncomfortable.

Don't hold grudges about their inevitable mistakes, and hope they will forgive you yours.

Ask their opinion or advice, just to see them glow in the light of equal or even superior status. After all, a good teacher is one who outmodes himself.

ELEVEN

Rebonding with the Young Adult

Much has been said and written about the disintegration of the modern family. Even though the closely knit network of relatives that past generations enjoyed is now largely absent, we believe that parents love their children as deeply as ever. The bonds of family care, concern, and abiding love are sustaining forces which give life meaning. The generation continuum, as parents watch children grow into adulthood—becoming responsible people with careers, marriage, and parenthood—gives an order and sense to life.

Although parents' bonds to their offspring are never totally broken, children, during the years of adolescence, disconnect their bonds in their quest for autonomy. Once adolescents feel secure as their own persons, they become receptive to reestablishing closeness with their parents. In order to have reached a stage of maturity wherein they feel inner strength, independence, and consistent and sure identity, late-adolescents have had to overcome childhood and leave it behind. Hopefully, in the course of this journey, the young person will have survived the lesson of life and retained a sense of curiosity about the future.

A young adult will have learned to give up the total self-absorption of the teen years in order to form intimate, long-lasting friendships and loves. Self-esteem will have become stable as the person has learned to build ethical systems based on loyalty, dependability, and social responsibility. Learning to deal with frustrations in solving problems has added to his or her maturity. Overcoming the loneliness of leaving home has fueled self-assurance. Decisions about life-style and career choice have made the young adult feel a sense of belonging to the "real" world, where options and decisions are important.

This psychological stance allows the young adult to let go of the period of disenchantment with parents. This letting go can happen at any time during late adolescence, depending on the person's emotional maturity. Adult children can then shed the narrow view of parents as controlling, superior people and begin to appreciate the breadth of their entire personalities. When this process begins, parents must also learn to enlarge their perceptions and treat offspring as complex persons, rather than simply as "my children."

A woman complained of her worries about her twenty-three-year-old son. He was a frustrated screenplay writer. His agent believed in his talents and, although the son was financially unsuccessful, had faith in the young man's future. The mother complained, "I keep telling him to stop being a hermit, writing his young life away. I want him to get out and have some fun. He's so serious about his work and won't consider anything else." This woman wanted her son to be happy, but on her own terms. He defined his life as worthwhile because he was involved with his creativity. He didn't want to become a part of superficial socializing and felt compelled to continue pursuing his craft.

We suggested that perhaps if the mother saw him as a unique, special person who must live differently from her, using his solitude to his own advantage, she might relax and wish him well.

"You mean accept him for himself and stop pushing my view of life on him?" she asked.

"Exactly."

The Door to Rebonding

The door that leads to rebonding will be entered happily by young adults when they are assured of acceptance as themselves, not as children who must fit into parents' expectations and dreams. This open attitude requires tact and vigilance on the parents' part. Years of giving advice, asking probing personal questions, and judging children's performances make these unwanted invasions seem automatic to parents—almost like a right that comes along with parenthood. These devices must be forever shelved if parents seek to rebond with their grown children.

In order for the reconnection to take place, parents and offspring must decide if they like each other. Would a friendship be possible if parents and grown children met as strangers? Are both parties flexible enough to respect each other's differing opinions and life-styles? Do they appreciate each other's strengths and forgive each others' weaknesses?

"I always loved my mother, but during our abrasive years, I didn't like her at all," reports a young woman. "It wasn't until I left home and ran my own life that I could see her as a likeable person. I had no idea what a sense of humor she possessed until we happened to be invited to the same party. People my own age were listening and laughing with her as she told funny stories about her job. I started to listen as a person, rather than as her daughter, and really could see her as a bright and witty woman. It dawned on me that my own overview of life was the same as hers. I had identified with her askance view of people's defenses, without being aware of incorporating her abilities of delivery and mimicry. As an independent person, I felt no threat to my sense of being myself when I reached the insight that I was like her in this respect."

She became friends with her mother, and more than normal pals. "When you get close to a parent, those old bonded feelings are so deep that the closeness is infused with comfort. You have memories which link you together, good and bad ones. Our joining as adult friends is precious to both of us. We never question loyalty, motivations, or honesty, because we have the foundation of family to work from. I had already rebonded with my father, since we didn't seem to have gotten in each other's way as my mother and I had. It really felt wonderful to be tight with both of them."

When offspring feel parents accepting them as individuals, they become extremely curious about the parent as a person with experiences, wisdom, and information to pass on.

A father related that during the years when his son was sixteen through eighteen, he kept telling him about the important matters of life. "I wanted him to know how to judge people, handle money wisely, and how to behave with women. He listened patiently, but he didn't really hear me. I was always frustrated, as he seemed to disregard my sound advice. He left home, got into incredible debt (which took three years to bail out of), got married and botched that up because of his selfishness, and couldn't hold a job. I thought he was a failure. He must have felt bad, too, because aside from occasional letters and phone calls at holidays, I didn't see him for three years.

"Now twenty-two, he came to visit me this summer. He wanted to know about how I see life. He asked me questions about everything that I had already told him when he was seventeen. Now, he really needs to know. I had wasted both his time and mine trying to pass on my philosophy when he wasn't ready for it. Now we disagree and we debate—and we love the dialogue. I never knew a father could become buddies with a child. He tells me that all his mistakes made him grow up. The main thing is that we really like each other. I feel stupid to have judged him, but glad I never voiced my opinion."

A young mother told us how she appreciates her mother's respect for her individual self. "When I had my first child, mother took a vacation from her work and came to help out. I was a little leery because she had always been kind of bossy. She arrived and, to my surprise, treated me as an equal. We talked about motherhood and her experiences with babies. All the time she was unobstrusively teaching me easy and joyful ways to take care of her grandson. I was an eager student, mostly because she wasn't giving orders or making judgments. We reunited, and now I feel like she's an older, wonderful sister to me."

As the young woman spoke, her mother's eyes glistened with happiness. "I *was* a bossy mother. I had three children to raise on my own, a tedious job, and lots of interests of my own. I felt like a commander of a ship, issuing orders on the run. When my daughter asked me to help out with her firstborn, I felt honored. I made a pact with myself that I would give her emotional support and help out with the physical chores, but I would treat her as a responsible, intelligent woman. I promised myself never to criticize her efforts, just as I would maintain silence about my friends' deficiencies. She needed a loving helper, not an imperious mother."

Rewards of Parenting

The rewards of parenting revolve around being needed, expressing love with children, and protecting and guiding them through their years of physical and emotional development. Since parenting is usually a chosen job, expecting gratitude for the burdens of raising children only leads to bitterness. Parents who demand respect, obedience, and appreciation from young adults end up lonely; whereas parents who take pleasure in the individual whom they have helped guide into adulthood rebond with their offspring. Whatever they may become, children retain needs for parental affection, praise, and encouragement. Mature offspring also recognize that their parents need the same emotional flow of love in return. They feel at ease giving love when they are treated as individuals.

"My daughter and son-in-law live on a working farm, raising goats and vegetables," states an urban woman. "At first, when they began their back-to-basics living style, I felt offended because they seemed to be giving up so much without a thought. They wouldn't be using their college educations, they would have little cultural stimulation. I worried about lots of things which were none of my business. But now I see that they are joyful people. They love their life and each other. She lives like I taught her—enjoy life—so I'm delighted for them." This parent has resolved her need to control, or interfere in, her daughter's choices. By so doing, she reaps the reward of participating in her child's happiness.

If Reconciliation Fails

If you feel your independent children still distance themselves from further emotional contact, examine why the family bond is broken. Do you still relate to your grown children as if they belonged to you, not to themselves? Do you try to tell them what to do with their lives? Do you become defensive if they seek to discuss parenting faults? Do you try to manipulate their love by using guilt as a lever? Do they take you for granted and still expect you to take care of them? Do they respect your privacy? Can they take your opinions into account?

If you unconsciously find yourself still wearing the old hat of possessive parenting, make a concentrated effort to change your approach. Admit that your habitual role is unworkable, and try to accept the boundaries between yourself and the unique person who once was your responsibility. Value the difference between yourself and your offspring as the result of normal evolutionary changes from generation to generation. Investigate how your expectations may not match up with your child's plans. Accept the fact that he or she is still a growing person with private hopes and dreams. Giving up rigid relating patterns leads the way to mutual respect and the gift of bonded love.

If grown children still expect you to take care of them as dependents, financially or emotionally, you must state your independent needs for freedom. If they take advantage of your good nature or hospitality, you have the right to demand proper manners and respect, just as you would from any other adult.

Security for Both Generations

When rebonding occurs between parents and young adults, a feeling of accomplishment settles around the relationship. Rebonded parents feel a sense of security that they can depend on their children's love in times of stress. Grown children feel safer in the world when they have emotional ties with the previous generation.

If you use common sense in parenting, the years of living with teenagers are later rewarded by mutual commitments of unconditional love and care.